Created to inspire and help table tennis players to improve their game.

ISBN: 978-0-9852884-0-2

Published by Table Tennis Achievements Publishing

Edited by Don Eminizer

Cover art by Nick Munson

www.breaking2000.com

Available as eBook for Kindle

Breaking 2000

by Alex Polyakov

Table Tennis Achievements Publishing

Foreword

I would like to tell you a little bit about Alex as a player. For the most part, he is like most table tennis players. However, looking at his accomplishments and seeing him achieve so much in a little over two years, it is obvious that he is gifted with a great deal of talent. Certainly he works hard, but even with the intense training he has received one would find that the outcome of the hard work would vary from person to person and not everyone would be capable of producing the same results.

Alex is passionate about table tennis; he trains hard and studies the game in very fine detail. Although at times his intelligence gets in the way, and leads him into too detailed thinking mode during the game, he is forever learning and that is what I really like about him as a player and an athlete.

I deeply respect and recognize Alex's competitive spirit as he never tries to shy away from competing in tournaments, including large 3-5 star events. He prepares for his tournaments and win or lose puts his skills to the test. To this day, he has always achieved something during every tournament. Each and every competition became a stepping stone to further development and improvement of his skills.

Coaching Alex reaches far beyond the table tennis court. We have achieved a great understanding of our minds. On the court however, he never seems to stop challenging me to excel as a coach while he strives to excel as a player.

When he embarked on the journey to document

his training, thoughts, disappointments and accomplishments, I knew he would be able to produce a great book. As I have expected, he was able to create the book that contains valuable information and is very easy to read. I especially like the way it leads from beginner to intermediate levels. Anyone who has played table tennis would be able to relate to some if not all of the experiences described.

I highly recommend this book to all of the beginners and developing players. I feel that every beginner in table tennis and every table tennis player that is struggling to improve through the intermediate levels of table tennis should read this book at least twice.

-- *Coach Gerald Reid*

Preface

There are many books on table tennis available on the market. Some explain the game and rules, others technique and training, but none of the books I've seen really go into any kind of detail explaining how to develop your game from a beginner to an advanced player. For that matter, no table tennis book shares a story of one's journey through that progression describing player's troubles and the improvements, the dedication and hard work. No book on table tennis gives readers a truly in-depth view at the challenges involved in becoming an advanced player, challenges that go a lot further than learning, techniques and practicing regularly. Yes, there is material out there on techniques that one must possess in order to become an advanced player; however, as I found out throughout my own journey, there are many other intangible skills that must be developed in the game – the so called game within the game.

When I started to play table tennis, I, just like many other table tennis amateurs, excitedly looked for any information that might help me to improve my game. Desperate for advice, I looked everywhere for answers to my questions. If you are an aspiring table tennis player, you undoubtedly have your own questions. In my case, I had a goal to break a ranking of 2000 set by the United States Association of Table Tennis (USATT), reaching a level of an advanced table tennis player. My main questions were what do I have to do to become a USATT 2000 level player? How do I improve?

Now, over two years into my table tennis training, I decided to write this book explaining how I've crossed the magic USATT 2000 mark. I am certain that this book will become an asset to every aspiring table tennis player's library as I share my experiences, my frustrations, and the valuable lessons I have learned along the way.

I am forever grateful to my coach, Gerald Reid, for his hard work and dedication to me as a student. His knowledge, experience, and training have been valuable assets that have allowed me to attain my goals.

How it all began

Two events brought on by faith led to my involvement in table tennis. First came in a form of a table tennis table a co-worker donated to the workplace. The second was an ankle injury I suffered during one of my Sunday indoor volleyball games.

The local YMCA where I played volleyball hosted a table tennis club whose players met and played games in a recreational room next to the gym. My ankle was still healing, preventing me from taking part in my weekly volleyball games, but I still wanted to get some exercise. I was already playing table tennis with my co-workers prior to sustaining my volleyball injury. On my way to the volleyball court I stopped in front of the table tennis hall as if I was standing at a crossroads and decided to go in to play table tennis instead. I had no idea that I would become so magically enchanted by this wonderful game.

On that special day, I managed to beat two players who, I thought, were incredibly tough. Both matches were close, but my game prevailed. I was happy and proud. I thought I was good. Hell, I thought I was *real* good. The following Sunday, disappointment struck. I played better players who beat me badly and laughed at my default. While the "laugh" may be an exaggeration on my part, the winning players definitely greeted my losses with a smirk. Match after match, I was unable to beat these players. They were obviously much better than I. They toyed with me. They were in full control of the game. They had an antidote to my every sting.

I can't say that I did not deserve a beating. I thought I was a good player. In hind sight I was perhaps a bit too arrogant. I can now see that my wins were the result of mere talent, since I did not at the time possess a single element of technique, nor did I have a very good understanding of the game. Yet the losses became a turning point. They made me realize that I wanted to improve in order to stand up to the better players. I wanted to learn to play in order to win.

One day, I arrived to the YMCA eager to challenge anyone willing to play against me. Ivan, a nice older gentleman, whom I played with all the time came up to me and said "Hey, there is a fantastic player in the other room. He is amazing. His name is Jerry, and he is a 2400 level player. Go ask him to play." Intrigued, I went next door, where I found, sitting along the table, a gentleman in his mid forties. He did not look like a great player. Actually, he did not look like a player at all. He carried a few extra pounds, lacking the stereotypical athletic physique I was imagining. With the thick glasses and baseball cap, gym pants and a long tee shirt, he looked more like a spectator than a player.

I asked him to play and we began our match after a short warm up. He did not do anything magical, but somehow I just could not hit the ball. He looked slow, and did not really move at all, yet I was only able to score the points when he dared me to hit the ball really hard. To my amazement, when I took my shots, the ball came back on the table!!! I swung at the ball harder and harder until I missed. Jerry returned all my shots.

I later found out that Jerry's 2400 level was a bit

of exaggeration on Ivan's part, yet Jerry's game was so great that he may as well have been at that level. Nobody at the club could beat him.

Two games later, without finishing our match, Gerald, or "Jerry" as Ivan called him, offered to show me how to hit the ball properly. This is how Gerald became my long time friend and a coach.

Becoming a serious player

Volleyball quickly became an activity of the past. I guess I was never partial to team sports -I wanted to be like a fighter ace in the days of World War I – to fight fairly, one on one against an opponent until the best man won.

Now that I had found a coach, new opportunities opened up to me. My sight was set on becoming the best player at my club. I needed to prove myself. I needed to gain the respect of better players in my club.

I started to train once a week for an hour. Two weeks later, after a heated discussion with an advanced player over what would be my USATT tournament rating, I signed up for a table tennis tournament in Drexel University. I argued that my game was good enough to be a 1500 level player. I was expecting to win every game in my groups - which were Under 1400 and Under 1550 sections.

I asked Gerald to help me prepare for the tournament and we agreed to increase the training to two one-hour sessions a week.

Prior to the tournament, Gerald and I have been working on countering the ball on the forehand and looping – something I could only do away from the table. The counter was a simple shot that I could use in succession. The loop, however was quite a wild shot. I was only capable to loop the ball far from the table as if I was scooping the ball from the floor. I also could only execute this shot by exerting a lot of speed and power. Without fast rotation of good power, the ball had no momentum or spin. It simply fell to the ground. What else could I have expected with only a few lessons under my hat? The tournament became a test – a test of my current game as I knew it, armed with my basic skills boosted up by few recent training sessions.

> **"I know exactly how I won and lost my matches during the tournament. I simply did not know what I did not know. My game consisted of simply reacting to the ball and hitting it if the opportunity came up. I had no strategy, no clear and concise thinking; all I had was a simple brute force."**

I came down with flu a few days before the tournament. I was afraid to miss the chance to compete, but the morning of the tournament I felt a bit of relief. I quickly packed my bag and drove down to the university gym. Unfortunately the relief was temporary. Few hours after arrival, the sickness returned. Yet, even playing sick I was able to come in with a 4-2 result. My initial rating became USATT 1284. Not a disappointment by all means, but not a result that I found satisfying either.

I know exactly how I won and lost my matches during the tournament. I simply did not know what I did not know. My game consisted of simply reacting to the ball and hitting it if the opportunity came up. I had no strategy, no clear and concise thinking; all I had was a simple brute force. At this level, the player who attacks first usually scores the point. In my case, the attack was only made possible when my opponent made a mistake and popped the ball up high above the net. This made the matches quite stale. Two players were simply bouncing the ball to each other waiting for their opponent to screw up and hoping not to be the first to make a mistake.

My first tournament helped me understand how difficult it really is to win a competitive table tennis match. Tournament jitters, new opponents, faster tables, many distractions, and pressure are elements that I had not previously considered. Nevertheless, I had my goals. The day I looked up my tournament results, I made up a goal – to reach USATT 2000 in a year. I asked Gerald, point blank "Do you think I can be over USATT 2000 in a year"? His answer was simple: "All you have to do is work hard and time will tell".

It took me two years and four months…

www.breaking2000.com

The goal or the challenge

I am certain that most of the table tennis players in local table tennis clubs have similar stories about how they began to play table tennis. I have not yet met a player who planned to be an advanced table tennis player without going through this trial period. It is mesmerizing to see the ball arch with the spin diving in a loop or experience the stress relieving feeling smashing a high ball. It is also every player's desire to beat their peers that drives one to develop a stronger game, to practice, and to learn new skills.

As I focused on my goal, I began to seek reassurance amongst other players whether or not I was capable of achieving what I had set out to do. On the Internet, I posted numerous questions on various table tennis forums. Could I truly become a USATT 2000 level player? I did not have doubts, but I was seeking support.

Several responses I received were encouraging – some coaches offered an advanced training method that guaranteed to develop a junior player to a USATT 2000 level within two years. However, these encouraging responses were more the exception than the rule. Most of the time, the responses were along the line of "you are out of your mind". What I found out is that there are dozens, even hundreds of players who never exceed USATT 1500 even with high level coaches and a lot of training. There are even more players in the lower ranks, and still quite a lot of players that hang near the USATT 2000 mark without ever attaining it or crossing it. Why would I be an exception to the rule?

I was 28 years old when I started to seriously play table tennis, and I have had some notable advantages over other players. First, I was a ballroom dancer from a very young age which would prove to be a huge help in developing my footwork and balance. My athleticism and excellent coordination also helped me succeed: even though being athletic does not guarantee success, it certainly did not hinder my progress. Finally, my thought patterns developed from the days when I competed in chess tournaments gave me a sound and solid mental base. Being an adult, I approached the training with my mind as much as my body, something that younger table tennis players often lack in the early stages of development.

With these tools in hand, Gerald and I began to work towards my goal.

Coaching methods

I cannot begin to stress the importance of sustained coaching in table tennis. Coaching has been the major factor in my success and is the biggest reason why I have been able to achieve my goals. Too many players tend to dismiss coaching and attempt to reach higher levels of game play on their own. I deeply respect these great individuals for their efforts and sheer willpower, but when it comes to table tennis, those who choose to proceed without proper coaching are taking the long route, and more often than not do not reach their full potential.

> *"The cost of learning the game without a coach is time – just how much time needs to be spent to reach desired results..."*

The most frequent reason players have been reluctant in securing a coach is because of the expenses associated with the process. This can be quite a surprise to some readers, but table tennis can indeed be quite an expensive sport. Yet, there is no price tag that can be set on time. Any aspiring player without the coach can conceivably achieve high levels of game play, providing they have the necessary time to dedicate to training. The cost of learning the game without a coach is time – just how much time needs to be spent to reach desired results depends on each individual player.

All coaches are different. Some coaches used to be great players and chose to become coaches when their career slowed down. These coaches were usually coached by somebody else and the school of thought has been handed down through many generations of formal training. These coaches follow a tradition that they themselves have come to embrace during their training and playing days. Other types of coaches are thinkers. They may have played the game, but not to the level of success to be recognized. Yet, they are considered good coaches because of their in-depth knowledge of every aspect of the game.

While Gerald is a highly regarded table tennis player in Philadelphia, he developed his skills on his own – through trial and error and hard work. He learned proper strategies in order to use his strengths in the game, and to minimize play against his weaknesses. He also developed an incredible knowledge and understanding of various playing styles. All of this knowledge built over years of experience, makes him a good coach. What makes him a great coach is the fact that his experience is combined with perfect mentoring style, charisma, and an almost Sherlock Holmes' observation and attention to detail.

> *"Gerald proposed to start by shaping my game in such a way that would allow me to develop certain undeniable strengths which would never fail me. ...Having this "base" would mean that these basic skills would in time become a power that would tilt the pendulum during my matches against ninety five percent of opponents of my level."*

When I mentioned my goal, he immediately began to tailor a customized training plan. It was obvious that in order for me to attain the level of USATT 2000, I needed to possess all the shots that a USATT 2000 player has mastered, all the control that a USATT 2000 player can muster, and all the footwork, coordination, and other necessary skills that a USATT 2000 player must possess.

Gerald proposed to start by shaping my game in such a way that would allow me to develop certain undeniable strengths which would never fail me. He called it a "base". Having this "base" would mean that these basic skills would in time become a power that would tilt the pendulum during my matches against ninety five percent of opponents of my level. This so called "base" was meant to establish a set of technically correct strokes, which I could execute flawlessly and with consistency.

A good technical foundation is the main reason that allowed me to propel quickly through the beginning ranks, but at the time the training plan was hatched neither Gerald nor I could foresee the results.

With an established training plan, the training intensified.

Forehand development

When anyone new enters a table tennis club, the first thing they see is forehand shots. Strong, powerful, "loaded" with spin – everyone must master this shot in order to advance. This shot stands out as the player is able to hit the ball harder and sharper, either away or right "through" the opponent. The question is, if everyone has developed these shots, what makes one player's forehand better than another player's forehand, and how do you develop a forehand shot that can successfully win points, games, and sets?

These are all important questions as the ground work of technique is being set in stone. Poor technique cannot be used with great success, while great technique cannot be taught all in one day.

Keeping up with my aggressive goal, Gerald decided to follow a layered development of my technique. The compromise was to develop a technique that can easily evolve and be improved upon with minor adjustments. Each of these adjustments will be gradually adopted by me into building a more threatening, deadly weapon.

Even though the future showed that introduction of the change initially had an adverse impact on my game, I am glad to note that this effect was only temporary. In the long run, Gerald's plan worked like a charm.

Prior to formal training, my forehand shot was a simple flat hit that sent the ball into the net half the time. Gerald and I began working on my forehand technique by converting my current forehand shot into a stable counter. I practiced the forehand counter for about a month, until I was able to execute the shot with high speed and accuracy. The goal was to repeat this shot numerous times in the row without fail.

It was quite a challenge to pass the "exam". I had to make 50 shots in the row at the same pace without missing. If I hit the ball wildly to the other side of the table, we had to start the test all over again. Did I mention that 50 times meant only counting the times when I made contact with the ball? Certainly not an easy task for a new player, but I eventually succeeded and was very happy that I mastered the first skill of table tennis.

Practicing this very basic skill brought several new discoveries. I finally understood the concept of the rhythm of table tennis - the sound you hear frequently walking into the training hall. The ball, sounding like a heart-beat, consisting of a two distinct quick double beats - sounds of the ball making contact with the paddle, then the table, then the sound of the same contacts from the training partner. The second concept was the use of speed. I could now hit the ball a little slower and still manage to send the ball over the net. I also noticed that I was able to slightly steer the ball to the same spot on every shot. Both of these discoveries helped me pass my test and move on to the next step.

The next step was to master an attack of an underspin ball on the forehand side. This meant using my forehand in order to lift and loop the underspin ball any time the opponent placed a back spinning ball on the forehand side of the table. I've never been able to do this shot in the past. I had to resort to pushing or dinking this ball back.

Learning this stroke was difficult, but Gerald was confident that I could figure it out. I was used to forehand countering which I practiced on prior to learning this skill. I was used to making contact to the back of the ball. Contacting the back of the ball sent the ball into the net. I was not producing sufficient spin to create the lift necessary to loop the ball over the net and onto the table. Gerald kept showing me how to contact the bottom of the ball and use the wrist to produce spin, but it was far too difficult. Nevertheless, neither of us gave up. While I managed to return one shot every once in a while, Gerald kept adjusting my wrist position until I was able to contact the bottom of the ball.

I was focusing heavily on applying wrist motion, but the timing of catching the ball in the right spot while synchronously using the wrist to generate spin was very poor. A few times, I managed to execute the stroke correctly. This is when Gerald said "just throw your arm into the ball, and let your body do the rest." First shot, a whiff. I missed the ball completely. Second shot, boom! The ball hit the ceiling. "Darn, I hit the edge of the paddle", I said, a little disappointed. Third time was a charm. I looped the ball!!!! Fourth try, looped again!!! Fifth, yet again!!! I was finally getting a hang of it.

Soon afterwards, I could continuously loop an underspin ball and we would get into chopping rallies where Gerald would chop several balls in the row producing underspin, while I executed an attack against the chopped ball by spinning or looping it back. I did not even notice when Gerald began to chop the ball a little bit wider to either side of the table, as if he was simply a little off in his return shot. Without even realizing this I began making slight side steps gauging the distance to the ball in order to repeat my shot. Gerald's keen trick played an important role in my training. I was developing footwork while strengthening the technique of attacking an underspin ball.

My consistency on this shot continued improving with every training session. Once I was capable of comfortably attacking at least five underspin balls in the row, Gerald introduced a next element into my game - the use of a backhand.

Backhand development

Gerald was quick to note that at lower skill levels, where I was competing, very few people possess good backhands because everyone's training is set primarily on developing a strong forehand. If the opponents had good backhands, but a low player rating, they probably possessed weak forehands.

The task was simple. It was enough for me to develop a consistent backhand counter in order to provide some resistance to incoming shots on the backhand side. If I could execute a stable backhand and was able to warm up before the match with a solid backhand technique, then my backhand might not seem to be a weakness against most of my opponents. The plan was to continue working on the backhand side once we could see that the backhand lacked consistency or strength and made my further progress stagnant.

We worked on backhand counter for a few sessions until I could feel comfortable taking this shot. Gerald never intended to make my backhand a primary weapon at this stage of my game. The main weapon remained a forehand loop.

A push

Looking back, it was very obvious what Gerald was doing with his approach to training. Back then, however, it seemed as if I was simply learning a new shot. I remember him saying to me: "Alex, I know you will hate this training, but we have to do it. Trust me." So I was warned, and oh boy, was he ever right. I *really* hated that training.

Gerald was teaching me a proper push. Seriously, this has to be the most boring shot in table tennis - you stand close to the table and try to "dink" the ball back low over the net, so that it retains has some backspin. Of course, I felt like I would rather spend my time learning to hit the ball harder, but I surrendered to my coach.

> *"...the push will make my opponent push and that is when I should loop the ball..."*

I did not ask him why I needed to learn this shot until I perfected its execution from both sides – forehand and backhand. Finally, after weeks of working on pushes, I asked him: "Gerald, can we stop it with this training, I'm falling asleep." He smiled and said: "Sure, now that I'm confident that you are doing it well, we can stop." I replied: "Fantastic!! Why did we spend so much time on it anyways?" The simplicity of his answer shocked me. The pieces of my game were being put together even without my noticing. He said: "Are you good at attacking underspin with your forehand?" I said "Yes, test me!" He continued: "Well, when you played in the tournament last time, and you pushed, what did your opponents do?" "They pushed back", I quickly replied. He stopped for a moment as if looking for me to add something, then continued: "Exactly. And what shot did you just want me to test you on?" I looked at him, puzzled, and said: "So the push will make my opponent push and that is when I should loop the ball?" "Exactly!!!" said Gerald.

This was my first lesson in table tennis strategy – a strategy that is built over a very simple sequence of shots that frequently occur at lower levels of table tennis.

Breaking USATT 1400

I participated in several tournaments in a row, with different results. I learned that I had to get a better warm up at the table. I learned not to look at ratings and trust my skill - playing as well as I could. I also learned that I needed to rest well before each tournament.

As I was getting better acclimated to playing in tournaments, I kept on working with Gerald on solidifying my game. The final step we worked on was the 3rd ball attack. It was very simple. It was a way to combine the serve, push, and the attack of the push with my forehand loop. I had to learn to put these strokes together in sequence with a good transition and solid consistency. Gerald made sure to systematically target pushes to backhand, forehand and the middle of the table in order for me to develop the steps and consistency of attack against a push placed anywhere on the table. I served, returned serve with a push, and attacked the push over and over with great excitement – I was missing the ball less and less. It soon became time to put the practice to the test in a competition.

It took me four months to reach the ranking of USATT 1400. I jumped to this level after 150 point adjustment gained in a Maryland tournament. I played fourteen matches that day with only 3 losses. Two of the losses were against USATT 1700 level players. I played these advanced players very well, yet they were much too strong for me. However, I managed to beat my first USATT 1500 level player. Gerald played a trick on me when it was my turn to play him. He said he would record the scores for me and took the record sheet. Not having seen the score sheet, I had no idea of my opponent's rating until the match was over. Surprisingly, I beat him 3-0 – a true testament to my training and Gerald's coaching.

Gerald was absolutely correct. A good short serve welcomed a push, and at the level where I was playing, pushes are rarely taught. When they *are* taught, they usually are not practiced long enough to make a difference in player's game. Many players were content to push the ball around too many times, waiting for their opponent to push the ball off the table or to put the ball into the net. So while my opponents were playing cat and mouse pushing the ball to each other, I was ready to attack. At USATT 1500 level, very few people are capable of blocking a well executed loop and since I had, as Gerald described, "power to spare" in my forehand loop, this made my shot even more fearsome. Point after point, I was able to repeat my deadly sequence and win my matches.

www.breaking2000.com

> *"Instead of focusing on attack shots, I found a weakness in my opponent's attack against my push... I was able to win the game using the strategy that I had developed within the game."*

This tournament also brought about another turning point which further enriched my skill level. As I was playing a lot of matches that day, I eventually found myself with very little energy left to continue playing. I got in trouble playing a lower rated player. I was not aggressive enough because I was tired, both mentally and physically. Instead of focusing on attack shots, I found a weakness in my opponent's attack against my push following several directional pushes. I was able to win the game using the strategy that I had developed within the game. I won that game and came up to Gerald, he pointed it out: "Nice job moving him around. Glad you found it on your own."

I was overjoyed that day. It was a serious breakthrough. What I did not know at the time is that only two months later, I would be taking another jump over the USATT 1500 mark and straight into USATT 1600.

USATT 1600

I continued to train with Gerald twice a week on the same elements – 3rd ball and underspin attack. Meanwhile, I continued to participate in tournaments. During one of the tournaments, I advanced to the final of Under 1700 Giant Round Robin event where my opponent was an older gentleman with slow movements and a rather strange game.

I was set to win easily until the game began. My opponent was using long pips as I later found out. My strong attacks and pushes had an adverse affect to my usually strong game. I missed almost all of my shots, whether they were pushes or loops. I was extremely frustrated and lost without being able to put up a fight. I was so upset that after the game I said to Gerald, almost stuttering: "His game… It's not table tennis!" Gerald looked at me, smiled and said: "And now we enter the next stage of our training. It is time to work on pips."

According to Gerald's analysis, I was capable of initiating my offense well enough to beat USATT 1500 level players on this skill alone, but I had no answer against a pip game because I had no feeling of a slow game nor did I have a good understanding of the long pip's effect on the ball. I was unaware that a long pip player cannot push; he *must* return either a no spin or a top spin ball as the response to an underspin ball. However, when a long pip player receives a topspin ball, he can return a no spin or underspin ball.

> *"Pay attention in the pre-match warm up and look at player's equipment in order to be on the look out for a tricky game."*

With such a wide variety in pip opponent's responses, I needed to learn to pay attention to opponent's response, as well as recognize in the warm-up whether the opponent is using so called "junk" rubbers - rubbers that do not react strongly to an incoming spin. Gerald also pointed out that from now on I must pay even more attention in the pre-match warm up and look at player's equipment in order to be on the look out for a tricky game. I also needed to pay more attention during a service return as different sides of the paddle can be used to serve the ball and produce a different type of a spin with the same service motion.

This was a lot of information to digest. Most of this information was theoretical and required experience playing other pip players in order to learn how to beat them. However, every player uses pips differently, so I needed to acquire the knowledge and then learn to adjust my strokes in the game depending on the type of ball produced by the opponent.

When I showed up for training the next day, Gerald reached into his bag and pulled out a paddle with short pips. We began working on the same exercises as before – pushing, looping against a push, and a 3rd ball attack. This time, he used the pip side of the paddle to respond to my shots and I needed to adjust my strokes to the type of ball produced by his equipment. Frequently, we divided our lessons into two parts, where I would first workout against an inverted rubber, and then switch and work against pips or first trained against pips and then switched to inverted. Since pips do not produce as much spin as inverted, all strokes needed to go through constant adjustments.

> **"...most players using pips or anti rubbers are relying on their opponent to miss – they want the opponent to attack harder and stronger until they miss."**

Some of these adjustments were difficult to get used to at first. For example, a push with pips produces very little spin while a push with inverted had a lot more spin on the ball. It took me a while to remember that if I pushed a ball pushed with pips, it had less spin, launching the ball up in the air for the opponent to kill. Nevertheless, in due time, I began to learn to adjust to an incoming ball and to recognize slight variations of spin that were produced by different type of equipment.

The following month I had to face the same player again in another tournament. This time I was ready for a rematch. I did not underestimate him this time, nor did I consider his game to "not be table tennis" any more. In Gerald's words, most players using pips or anti rubbers are relying on their opponent to miss – they want the opponent to attack harder and stronger until they miss. This allows them to use the full power of "junk" rubbers. However, what they are also showing you is that they are hiding a weakness. Their weakness is their constant need to slow the game down in order to have more time to respond to incoming shots. Usually, this is done in order to have time to protect one of the sides of their play – the side that they are less consistent with.

With this strategy in mind, I started my game. Ten minutes later, with a spring in my step, I was walking to the tournament director with a winning score sheet. My opponent was shocked. Only a month has gone by, but I was a different player. My scores in the match were reversed to the scores of my last loss against the same opponent. This time, however this player was rated over USATT 1600.

In addition to beating a long pip blocker, I had beaten a high USATT 1500 level player and another USATT 1600 level player. I also had four losses to higher rated players from USATT 1600 to USATT 1800 with a score of 3 games to 2, which was another accomplishment of its own.

En route to USATT 1800

I wish I could say that my progress continued without obstacles, but that is not how it happened. After I hit the USATT 1600 mark for the first time, I had some great successes and some failures. The game changed more than ever before. The opponents became more consistent. Opponents' styles became more diverse, requiring new strategies and tactics to be used in the game. Up to that point, I had been able to win using the same pattern over and over without much resistance. At the new higher level, my opponents were able to set up and initiate their attacks with as much consistency as I. I had to learn when and how to defend. My touch also needed to improve for service returns as the opponents were more ferocious in attacking weak service returns.

> *"Since this was the shot that caused me to lose more points, Gerald began to teach me how to defend on my weaker - backhand side."*

My opponents and their coaches were quick to recognize the lack of defense and stability on the backhand side. I could no longer bluff having a strong backhand. As soon as the first attack was guided towards my backhand and scored an immediate point for my opponent, my backhand became the target of constant and relentless abuse. Since this was the shot that caused me to lose more points, Gerald began to teach me how to defend on my weaker - backhand side. The exercise was simple, but very important. Gerald took a step or two back from the table and began looping to my backhand. I was learning to block the loops back.

A seemingly simple exercise, it is frequently overlooked by many developing players for similar reasons as pushing. Players spend more time developing weapons where they can hit the ball harder and faster, but fail to win points using their new weapons during the match due to the glaring weaknesses in the other areas of the game. What I have learned when I reached USATT 1600 is that a strong attacking shot does not guarantee a win. A simple strategy of merely preventing the opponent from executing his best shot leads to a completely different result of a match. I learned this very quickly by observing more experienced opponents changing their strategy in the game to stay away from my forehand, completely taking away my initiative. I was eager to eliminate backhand as an obvious weakness in my game.

> **"Because I missed the backhand block so many times, I was afraid to make mistakes and tapped the ball very gently without reading the spin on the incoming ball and adjusting the angle of the paddle accordingly."**

Prior to backhand block training I was too slow to block incoming loops on the backhand side – I never seemed to be ready for them either mentally or physically. Seeing a loop launched into my backhand, I reacted with indecision, going against Gerald's main rule – "there is no hesitation of table tennis". Because I missed the backhand block so many times, I was afraid to make mistakes and tapped the ball very gently without reading the spin on the incoming ball and adjusting the angle of the paddle accordingly. Slow reaction and fear of spin caused me to make more mistakes in the process. I kept increasing the angle of the block, overcompensating for all the times that I blocked the ball into the net, frequently sending the ball off the table.

As the training progressed, first signs of improvement were quick to come about. My control on the backhand block improved. I was only able to block a loop or two at first, but my consistency kept increasing. Only a few training sessions helped me significantly improve this shot. Since Gerald is right handed, he expanded my block training by looping to me using his backhand. A right handed player's backhand loop has some element of side spin, similarly to the left handed player's forehand loop. This taught me how to read the spin and apply my backhand block against a wide variety of attacking shots. Furthermore, Gerald expanded my blocking training by looping to me not just from the backhand side of the table, but also from the forehand corner. This allowed me practice blocking loops that were aimed down the line.

In few weeks, I was able to do a lot more with the ball. I developed the feel to block the ball softly, as well as to block the ball hard – with somewhat of a punch. This training developed another intangible skill – it significantly reduced the fear of incoming loops. Now I was capable of responding quickly and efficiently to an offensive shot to my backhand. While I still made mistakes on the backhand block from time to time, my backhand no longer looked as an easy target for my opponents.

In addition to my regular training lessons with Gerald, I continued to strengthen my strokes by training with a robot. I kept my robot training simple:

by setting it to produce long underspin balls to the middle of the table, while I looped the ball to either side. This allowed me retain the strength and consistency of my attacking game against an underspin ball while Gerald and I worked on something else.

After a few weeks of training, I played in one of the biggest tournaments on the east coast: the 2009 Eastern Open. During this tournament, I beat my highest rated opponent to date, a USATT 1850 rated player.

My results in this tournament were nothing to brag about. I only had one notable upset, yet it allowed me to see that my game had significantly improved. First, I was capable of blocking numerous attack shots on the backhand side; it was clear evidence that the backhand training was working. I also had great success against higher rated players. However, the greatest improvement visible was in the strengthening of my attacking game: 3rd ball attack and looping of underspin. While these were the very skills that allowed me to reach the USATT 1600 level, my shots during the tournament were much more consistent and a lot more powerful than ever before.

This tournament in addition to other local tournaments also identified new, easy to spot weaknesses. My service returns remained quite poor against serves with some element of sidespin. I did not react well to long underspin serves and kept pushing a long ball instead of attacking it. Additional weaknesses consisted of poor reaction to a flip on service return, unforced service errors, and poor mental preparation which caused me to play too safely in a close game with a stronger opponent, resulting in a loss of a match.

Finally, I lacked fluency transitioning from backhand to forehand side in order to attack or defend. Inability to combine or retain the attack using forehand and backhand in succession forced me to work extra hard to use my forehand, which frequently led to premature exhaustion during long rallies.

> *"The reason I had gaps in my game is because I lacked confidence in the use my backhand. I chose to run around my backhand instead, wasting energy with extra efforts and making my movements very predictable."*

Obviously, these weaknesses needed to be addressed if I was to improve further. With such a large list of items to work on, which element did we need to improve on first? Gerald's answer to my question was very concise and extremely simple. "Let us continue strengthening your backhand", he said.

The reason I had all these gaps in my game is because I lacked confidence in the use my backhand. I chose to run around my backhand instead, wasting energy with extra efforts and making my movements very predictable. I possessed good control of blocking, but did not know how to offensively attack a ball with my backhand.

On service return, I was only capable of attacking a long ball with a forehand. A long serve to my backhand was a clear set up point for my opponent as I rushed to pivot around the ball and use my forehand. Without being able to spin the ball with my backhand, my service return against long side spin and top spin balls toward the backhand was executed with a push – a shot that immediately gave my opponents an opportunity to attack.

Having been able to return serves with my backhand using spin, I would have also reduced the footwork necessary to continue executing offensive shots with my forehand. Thus, it came time to develop some offensive shots using my backhand.

I was very eager to eliminate my weaknesses and worked very hard during our sessions following the tournament. Gerald cleaned up my initial backhand strokes and tweaked my technique to produce topspin with my backhand counter until I was able to make 2 to 3 backhand loops in succession against different incoming loops. Then, we quickly moved on to the drills. At first, Gerald kept the drills simple: "We are always going to start with the backhand. I will roll the ball to you and you will counter it to my backhand. Then, I will block it to the middle of the table so you can hit it with your forehand to my backhand. Then, I will block it back to the backhand. We will do this over and over – don't swing too hard, you will need your energy."

Gerald was correct. I needed a lot of energy to get through this exercise. I was jumping for hours doing this drill. But I soon found that I did not have to focus as hard to perform it as the training progressed and I developed an improved reaction to different return shots. I was becoming very fast and my responses began to feel automatic – no thoughts, no hesitation. I also began to drive the ball with more power and spin.

I got so comfortable with this drill that I was able to converse with Gerald about strategies and different elements of the game while drilling. Meanwhile, my focus remained intact and I was able to carry on the drill and even fish out an occasional net or edge ball to continue it.

Then, Gerald began to teach me how to attack a long underpin ball with my backhand. "Once you have this shot, you will no longer need to play cat and mouse when you receive a push to the backhand. Remember, you must be prepared to attack first! That is the secret of your success!" I completely agreed as I recalled many rallies attempting to push opponents around in order to get a push that was in my forehand zone.

> *"At first, my biggest challenge was a floating starting position on the backhand. I simply did not have enough time to prepare for a backhand shot, as my ready stance was purely forehand oriented."*

This shot was just as difficult for me to learn as the attack of underspin on the forehand side. A lot of adjustments between the angle of the blade and point of contact of the blade with the ball needed to be made.

At first, my biggest challenge was a floating starting position on the backhand. I simply did not have enough time to prepare for a backhand shot, as my ready stance was purely forehand oriented. Transitioning from forehand oriented stance to execute the backhand affected my timing. Once Gerald corrected the ready position, I began making more progress but still made a lot of mistakes. Missing the ball completely and hitting the ball with an edge of the paddle was a common occurrence. Gerald kept tweaking my backhand bit by bit, but nothing seemed to help me achieve consistency. He admitted later that he was about to give up on teaching me this shot. "Perhaps backhand is not one of your strengths – there are a lot of people that play the game well without ever developing a good backhand against underspin", he thought to himself.

Then one day he came over to my side of the table and told me to execute my shot slowly several times in succession without a ball. What he found was astonishing. I was dropping my arm below the table on the ready position, hiding the true reason for my critical errors in timing. As I settled in the ready position and set my eye on the ball, my wrist slightly rotated, making the forehand side of the blade face the floor. With my blade forehand side of the paddle parallel to the floor, when I needed to execute the stroke, instead of making a single motion to bring my wrist back for a shot, I had to make two large motions to do so, resulting in a significant loss of time. Seemingly a fraction of a second is all it took to break up my consistency.

To eliminate my bad habit, Gerald served long underpin balls to my backhand, which I was to loop slowly. I was developing a new feel for a proper ready position. My backhand consistency improved almost overnight, taking my training to the next level – combining my backhand push and backhand underspin loop into a smooth and effective combination. Drills such as "Push, Push, Spin", where I was to vary the push and spin of the ball with my backhand as a response to an underspin ball became great tools in my training, as I was able to repeat the sequence of strokes over and over.

While I was learning new elements of the game, I continued to compete in various tournaments.

Breaking USATT 1700

I would like to point out the moment when I broke USATT 1700 for the first time. During the tournament, I was able to take an early 2-0 lead in games against a USATT 1960 rated player. I was hoping to win sooner, but my opponent recovered and evened out the match at 2-2. Magically, I "woke up" in the last game, taking an early lead of 4 points. My opponent worked hard to catch up, but made a few mistakes that cost him the match.

I wish I could say that I was dominating the game, but I wasn't. My win was only possible thanks to the relentless backhand training. I saved many shots sent to my backhand. I also attacked an underspin ball very well on the backhand side applying heavy topspin. My opponent continued to dare me to use my backhand, but my consistency proved to be superior.

I gained confidence early in the match and reinforced it in the 5th and deciding game. One of the crucial mental reinforcements was a long rally which I won leading the score at 9-7. After an opening, I was attacked. My opponent kept looping to my backhand throughout the match and even though I blocked some attacks he scored many points using the same shot. I felt he was going to execute the same fierce shot again. I saw the opponents' backswing and backed off the table immediately. I guessed correctly: the opponent looped to my backhand. I had no time to react; my instinct took over. I threw my paddle forward in front of me with my wrist twisted to the forehand side to redirect the shot and instantly felt contact with the ball. The ball deflected with a strong sidespin into my opponent's backhand. As the ball hit the table, the side spin reacted and the ball jumped farther to the right. My opponent reached as far as he could but missed the ball completely. Now, the pressure was fully on my opponent while I had three match points to spare. I won that game in the next point.

Unfortunately, this match drained my mental and physical strength. Unable to recover and fully concentrate, I lost several matches to opponents I should have beaten. I played 14 matches that day - a clear indication that my stamina was not strong enough to sustain high level performance for a long period of time.

Yet, I was ecstatic. I had beaten a player nearly 300 points above my rating. My mental game showed significant improvement. I played my game with confidence. In addition, the results of the backhand block and backhand loop against underspin both during service return and as 3rd ball attack were clearly visible.

My coach and I celebrated in style that evening,

having dinner at a nice Italian restaurant and reviewing my games over a meal of pasta and chicken Parmesan - a celebration we indulge in to this day to mark my performance improvements and tournament accomplishments.

Renewed road-map to USATT 1800

I did not retain my rating over USATT 1700 for too long. I dropped back to a USATT 1600 rating after quite a few losses. While I was expecting to perform better after my recent success, new weaknesses in my game came out during subsequent tournaments that did not allow me to progress as I had hoped.

> *"I kept dropping my arm after looping underspin, executing the same stroke against a topspin ball as well – which sent the ball off the table. I was making the same mistake on the backhand."*

I was playing well when I was the first to initiate an attack and met passive resistance, but a mere active block or counter attack made my consecutive shots very inconsistent. Gerald noted that I kept dropping my arm after looping underspin, executing the same stroke against a topspin ball as well – which sent the ball off the table. I was making the same mistake on the backhand.

My performance was even worse when I myself was under attack. In a long rally, I jammed up and threw the ball on the table instead of continuing the execution of offensive shots. Once I began making mistakes and missing, I lost confidence in looping the ball. This lack of confidence had a huge impact my mental game. I felt jammed, locked. I stuck the paddle out to meet the ball and trap its motion, instead of working with the ball to counter it. I was simply not used to entering the rally and playing long rally points.

Further elements that needed improvement were service return of tomahawk serves, lack of adjustment attacking consecutive no spin balls and top spin balls, poor smashes against lobs, and poor strategy. This was yet another long list of items to work on. I kept documenting my feelings, strengths, and weaknesses after several tournaments in order to go over these items with Gerald and seek ways to continue improving.

Most of my issues in the topspin game were the result of playing too few of topspin attacking players. My home club mainly consisted of defensive players – long pip blockers, short pips and anti combination choppers, long pip choppers, and blockers with good attacking forehands. Therefore my exposure to practice against topspin players was minimal. When opponents in my club defended against my shots, I had more time to move my feet and get into position for a follow up attack. During the topspin game against a more aggressive player, the time to react and move into a position was reduced. In addition, I retained my position close to the table against choppers because my attacking shots forced them away from the table. I stepped back slightly after my shot to recover and evaluate where the returning ball would land, then stepped in again to make the next shot. Against an attacking player, this movement required me to be a lot faster – which I was not used to doing.

Faced with lack of experience in topspin counter play, I could not anticipate the depth and the amount of spin on the incoming ball and again began to hesitate. I lost such points more often than not.

To address newly found weaknesses, I stopped playing choppers as frequently as I had in the past and began traveling to other clubs in order to find competition among topspin players. In some busy clubs I was only able to play 3-4 matches an evening against topspin players, but even those few matches were sufficient to help me acquire necessary experience and exposure to that type of game.

Meanwhile, I continued to train with my coach. Gerald was quick to pin point the problem I was having with service return of the tomahawk serve. He noticed that I was attacking it as if it was an underspin ball, generating lift when there was no underpin to lift, sending the ball off the table. When I missed the serve several times in a row, I began being too careful with the serve, pushing it or slightly guiding it - the worst possible response to this type of a long serve since the heavy spin always reacts favorably to the opponent, launching the ball deep or simply resulting in an unforced error.

After several sessions, my return of the tomahawk serve began improving. We made sure to dedicate 15 minutes of every training session to executing a return of this service. In order to cover the basis of my responses, Gerald also made sure we covered the means to properly push this type of the serve. This was especially helpful when the serve was short.

Lob practice was very difficult. I learned to wait for the ball and improved my timing, but I truly learned to attack this defensive shot properly only several months later – when I had a chance to practice in a hall with a very high ceiling. However, even acquiring the feel for timing a bounce of the ball in a lob was sufficient to return the shot. I rarely smashed hard because spinning this ball was safer. I also accidentally came up with a windshield wiper sidespin loop against a lob which sent the ball to the side – a shot that reduced the possibility of a repeated return. Along with a safe drop shot, even though it was quite high, allowed me to combine the shots in a point winning sequence.

To improve my reactions and my focus during a long rally, Gerald and I worked on a forehand & backhand transition loops a few steps away from the table. This helped me develop a feel for the ball trajectory and its bounce at a farther distance. This was very helpful for backhand. I believe this exercise is what helped me acquire a good touch for an away from the table backhand loop.

I attended more tournaments. The results varied. I worked hard to eliminate my weaknesses, however in tournaments my weaknesses kept coming back. Gerald and I were getting quite impatient. I seemed to have everything I needed to advance to the next level and showed a lot of toughness during my matches. I pulled off some wins with great comebacks and I won several critical matches against improving players, effectively blocking their rating adjustments from taking place, but I did not produce significant rating increases for myself. I had a tendency to play certain games well and others very poorly – a typical trait of a so called "hot and cold" player.

"Looking at the trends of my matches, Gerald noticed a major element that contributed to my game instability... I relied heavily on the warm up preparation and my mental game strongly depended on it."

Looking at the trends of my matches, Gerald noticed a major element that contributed to my game instability. To gain confidence and readiness, I required a good continuous warm up for my tournament matches. This is quite a challenging task at a tournament since all tables are used for tournament matches and the few minutes between the matches allow little time for proper warm up. I relied heavily on the warm up preparation and my mental game strongly depended on it.

Gerald suggested that I stop warming up in club matches. Instead of doing so, my task was to simply stretch a bit before starting my game. This decision had a huge effect on my game: I learned to focus quickly and make adjustments in the game a lot sooner. For tournament play, this preparation method was invaluable. I stopped relying heavily on my tournament warm up and was able to get ready for a match well within the two minute warm up interval.

Back to USATT 1700

For several months I stayed in high USATT 1600 ratings, unable to advance. However, during the 2009 North American Teams Championships in Baltimore, I have beaten several players and broke USATT 1700 level again.

This tournament is known for upsets, but it's not the wins that I am mostly proud of. I was very happy to play evenly with USATT 1800 players. In the previous matches against USATT 1800 opponents, I looked and felt outclassed. Now, I was able to stand my own ground and exchange shots.

> *"It is a lot easier to fix timing on rushing shots because the feet are moving. It is a lot harder to make the feet move when they are not."*

I did get tight in close matches. I guess I wanted to win too much, but I did not lose due to jammed blocking as I had in the past. I simply rushed my shots – which was a significant improvement from previous games. It is a lot easier to fix timing on rushing shots because the feet are moving. It is a lot harder to make the feet move when they are not.

Overall, the tournament was a very pleasant experience. My team performed well and we advanced from our division to a division two places higher. We faced players around 100-200 rating points above us. Almost all games were close – requiring full concentration and strong mental game to win. I did not succeed in all my games, but I did not play defensively in deuce games, which was a new milestone in its own right. My mental toughness was building up. Personally, I kept repeating the same words to myself, like a mantra: "I would rather lose playing my game and missing, instead of not playing my game at all." This allowed me to focus on the deuce points as if the score was still 0-0.

> *"...if you play your game, you will someday improve. If you do not play your game, you will simply just play the same way not allowing the skills learned in training to flourish."*

One may say that it does not matter how you lose the games, that a loss is a loss no matter what. I disagree. I believe that it's best to lose the game by playing it your best way and missing, instead of playing a toned down and safe game and not fighting – completely surrendering the initiative to your opponent. After all, if you play your game, you will someday improve. If you do not play your game, you will simply just play the same passive way all the time

www.breaking2000.com

not allowing the skills learned in training to flourish.

I waited anxiously to find out my new rating after the tournament and was very happy to find out that I had gone up to mid USATT 1700 level rating.

Good bye USATT 1600

Table tennis requires strong mental skills, not only during the matches but also in training and in the development of a player's skills. I learned this the hard way.

> *"If you plan on becoming USATT 2000 level player, you must beat <u>everyone</u> under USATT 2000. If you want to stop dropping your rating points, you must beat everyone that has a rating lower than yours".*

My next few tournament results were very poor according to my own standards. With my promising achievements I have been able to accomplish up to that point I expected to beat USATT 1600 rated players easily, but instead found myself struggling. Yes, my rating was higher, but if I did not play the game hard and attack well, I became a weaker player. I was disappointed in my losses, especially since I knew exactly what would have allowed me to convert my losses to wins. Somehow during the game, I completely deviated or stopped playing *my* game. I simply struggled playing against players around my level.

> **"...I had to play all players under my level <u>harder</u> than I play anyone else."**

This was easily explained by Gerald. He said "If you plan on becoming USATT 2000 level player, you must beat *everyone* under USATT 2000. If you want to stop dropping your rating points, you must beat everyone that has a rating lower than yours."

This made perfect sense. He told me that I had to play all players under my level harder than I play anyone else. I must focus to win those matches just as hard as I focus when I play high rated players. I must close the games early, aiming for 3-0 wins, and I was not to experiment with my game or strategy unless I was leading the match 2-0.

In March 2010, eighteen months after I began my training with Gerald I broke USATT 1800. My rating never fell into USATT 1600 level again.

The new level

I found myself becoming a USATT 1800 level player. This was a great cause for celebration, especially because I have won some very tough matches in order to get there. I beat a combination player who used anti and smooth rubber, I won a match against a retriever, a type of style that I had struggled with in the past, and I had beaten every player whose rating was lower than mine as well.

Entering the new level, I embarked on a new journey. I stayed in USATT 1800 level for about the same time as I had remained in USATT 1600 level – about 10 months. A seemingly a small two hundred point difference in rating points consisted of skills that were imperative to my ongoing growth and the improvement of my game.

To break out of USATT 1600 level, I needed to improve my defense, my service and service return, as well as passive defense. In USATT 1800 level, the difficulty of the skills necessary to advance was a lot higher.

The main areas of my game that needed to improve were strategy and backhand use. It was no longer sufficient to serve anywhere and attack anything that came back with my forehand. My opponents became mentally tougher, tactically better, and had established skills to defend against my offensive shots.

Gerald and I had a long conversation on the priority of the skills I needed to improve upon or develop. I felt that my footwork on the forehand was lacking and wanted to work on the forehand; Gerald, however, explained the true reason I felt this way. Due to the lack of consistency and strength on my backhand side, I was forced to compensate certain shots with footwork. This was a very tough way to play table tennis. Yes, there are lots of players that choose to use strong forehand shots to win their matches, but these players stagnate as soon as they meet opponents with established skills in defense and placement control. In addition, the physical strength and cardio necessary to play high level table tennis at high speed is enormous for a forehand oriented player. This was leading me to quicker burnouts and energy laps during tournaments. Since my tournaments consisted of participation in several sections at the same time, I could not afford to choose such an aggressive and demanding style.

> *"...since I already worked on these items in the past, the analysis should have produced different weaknesses. However, the truth is that the weaknesses are very difficult to completely get rid of. In reality, the same weaknesses become visible again at a higher level."*

I hope you have noticed that the analysis of my game in this stage of my development was very similar to the analysis conducted by Gerald after I broke USATT 1600. It may seem that since I already worked on these items in the past, the analysis should have produced different weaknesses. However, the truth is that the weaknesses are very difficult to completely get rid of. In reality, the same weaknesses become visible again at a higher level, which is what began to occur again in my game. Hence, the same skills needed to be worked on to reach a new level of stability and consistency.

Gerald and I went back to basics. Emphasis was

placed on developing the stability and offensive strength of the backhand. I needed to attack underspin ball very well. This was the very shot necessary to open up the game at the earliest time during the rally. With a strong opening on the backhand side, I would be able to dominate an earlier start of the offense, hence taking decisive control of the rally.

This time, however, Gerald suggested changing the stroke by adjusting my backhand to drive the ball instead of spinning it – a skill we had worked on when I reached USATT 1600. My biggest challenge was to adjust my starting position for the stroke. Without a new starting position I was unable to make proper contact with the ball – I kept hitting the bottom of the ball and lifting it over the table, instead of making contact with the back of the ball and driving it forward with more pace and spin.

It took about a week to get used to the new starting position, but once I was able to focus and constantly set my wrist and arm in the same position prior to executing the stroke, my consistency skyrocketed. First, I made 20 shots in a row, then 30, 40, 50, and more. We even created a game where after initial warm-up and prior to starting our training, we spent 15 minutes to loop an underspin ball in succession. The goal was to execute 100 loops of an underspin ball in a row while Gerald chopped the ball back. Five balls were allowed to be missed to complete the game. This was exciting as my numbers began nearing 100 consecutive shots. The shots I missed were very few and acceptable due to the nature of the chopping game – some off the table chopping is quite difficult to return and if I missed a few (or 2.5 percent), we still considered being an excellent result. This meant I was ready to move on to the next phase of backhand development.

Strengthening my attack of underspin on the backhand side meant that I was able to open the rally well on the backhand side as a 3rd ball attack. The next step was to continue applying the pressure on the backhand side if the 3rd ball attack was blocked or countered back into the backhand. I needed to counter loop against a topspin ball with my backhand after a return of the opening on the backhand side. This required improving transition on the backhand side – reducing errors when forced to make attack against underpin followed by attack of the topspin in succession.

I was missing my shots frequently until I developed solid feel over the difference in the starting position for the different strokes. I had worked on this weakness in the past on the forehand side and that experience helped significantly when I worked at it on my backhand side.

My narrative might seem light on the description of the training of my backhand side, however it took over two months for me to learn and get accustomed to my new skills. Even when it seemed that I was ready to move on practicing a next set of skills, we again backtracked to the basics. The purpose was to solidify all that I had learned to date. In order to repeat the material in a more difficult setting, Gerald brought out the good old learning tool – his paddle with short pips.

We repeated the same exercises in small intervals varying the "opponent's" equipment. I was learning to make adjustments quicker. I was learning to read the ball. I was also learning to retain the pressure of my attack against a wide range of defensive shots.

More tournaments followed. The results were satisfactory – some areas of my game had improved, while another had started to decline, especially on the forehand. While I learned to attack and sustain attack on my backhand side, my forehand showed very little of the scoring potential as it had in previous matches. It was no longer a fearsome weapon.

I felt like my feet were not moving or at least not moving fast enough in order to execute a good forehand shot. I was too slow and unresponsive. I even began to miss forehand loops against underspin. I was disappointed. I did not want my game to fall apart. After expressing my concerns to Gerald, he explained: "Your brain cannot retain all of its past information, especially considering the new material we are learning. You will lose some of the skills while you are learning new skills due to the learning pace we've set. Don't be alarmed, you did not lose your old skills, they're still there. We just need to stimulate them again. You're doing great!"

This was true encouragement. To revive my past forehand weapons, we began to drill forehand and backhand transitions. The purpose was to engage backhand to the maximum to make it even more effective, while allowing the forehand to engage when the opportunity presented, therefore reviving my prior forehand attacking spirit on demand.

I wish there were enough words to express the feeling of yet another improvement resulting from such drills. My forehand shots came back with a vengeance.

My backhand was ticking like clockwork. In addition, something else came out during drilling. I now had a new forte – my backhand. I could rip the ball so fast, even Gerald was amazed. My forehand had found its match.

Gerald noted that my backhand produced a much stronger shot than the forehand. The backhand shot was much "heavier" in spin. It is also more difficult to read the amount of spin the ball carried in my stroke because of the pace and low trajectory of the shots coming from my backhand. Forehand remained strong due to good placement control, excellent speed variation, power, and consistency. Because of the difference in the effects my forehand and backhand had on the ball, if I was capable to deliver a mixed set of shots using forehand and backhand combinations, I could expect to take advantage of the point.

My new lows and highs

In the 6 months following breaking a USATT 1800 rating milestone for the first time, I played 91 tournament games. My results varied. I hit quite a few lows during this time by losing to a handful of low ranked players. However, I also achieved new highs by beating my first two USATT 2000 players.

Gerald looked at my results with excitement. "I am not concerned with the losses. You are dynamite on a time delay. It will blow up, but we just can't predict when. You show that you can completely dominate some players – you're on the right path." This was very true. I was training hard and playing well. The improvement took some time to build up and siphon into the tournament play. Even the better players around me began to notice the changes and invited me to play them in the club.

"I had to learn to recognize and attack loose serves, serves that trailed a little bit long or a little bit high. In addition, I needed to learn to attack certain serves viciously - especially if the serve was designed to force an attack."

In the meantime, Gerald and I continued to work on other areas of the game. Service return became the next skill to be addressed. I had to learn to recognize and attack loose serves, serves that trailed a little bit long or a little bit high. In addition, I needed to learn to attack certain serves viciously - especially if the serve was designed to force an attack. This meant attacking serves hard, varying the placement of the return.

Finally, we began to address the ultimate missing link in my game: the ability to counter loop. This was the first time that my lack of ability to counter loop became evident. In the past, a simple block was enough to keep the opponents at bay and force them to miss. I could block to redirect the ball to a spot where the next attacking shot was more difficult and therefore risky. I also knew how to counter over the table, but when caught away from the table my response was usually a simple roll back onto a table instead of moving up to the ball to deliver an offensive counter loop. This is exactly the shot my opponents wanted to receive to finish the point - a high ball with little spin placed in middle of the table. This type of return was crushed immediately 99 percent of the time.

Gerald and I began by taking a few steps away from the table and looping to each other back and forth. At first, I learned to deflect the ball with spin using the incoming spin and pace of the ball. I had a hard time adjusting to the bounce of the ball and its trajectory after a strong spin. I could not tell where to move, especially when faced with a side spun ball. Yet my coordination improved after a few weeks. Instead of using the incoming speed and spin, I learned to apply my own pace and spin on the ball in order to offensively drive the ball instead of simply returning it on the table. As my loops became stronger, Gerald's responses became stronger, challenging me further.

Soon, I learned to play the ball offensively even when I was attacked. I recalled all of the younger players that I had played in the past and recognized why I struggled against their game so much. I had only just developed a crucial counter looping skill, main element of which consisted of reading the path of the ball, its bounce, and its spin. Meanwhile, the younger players were taught this skill first and were happy when the game opened up into a counter looping rally.

Counter looping training improved my footwork. When Gerald and I began working on this skill, I looped and took a step back, looped again and took another step back until Gerald blocked the ball softer. The soft block significantly bothered me as I did not move forward well to keep attacking a shorter ball.

Instead I fished for the ball near the floor – a very weak, passive, and an unnecessary response. The training changed my reaction to this situation. I learned to move forward and backward with a lot more freedom, still retaining my posture and offensive opportunities.

Anxious to break USATT 1900

I had several tournaments planned and was anxiously waiting to break into USATT 1900s. My performance in several tournaments was good enough to break the next rating level; however that is not how it happened. I fell a few points short and remained in USATT 1890s for several months.

Oh what a feeling it is to feel that you have broken the barrier only to find out in the next rating update that you are still 10 meager points away from your goal! One of the tournaments I gained 7 more points, halting me three points away from USATT 1900 mark. I can only smile reminiscing about the mixed emotions going through my head. I knew I would eventually reach higher – I was prepared to play and I was ready to win. I felt like I had already broken the next level. But those pesky three little points were still eating at me to some extent.

You might be wondering why I felt like I had broken through to the next level despite my rating. That was my feeling after attending the North American Team Championships in November 2010. Only the previous year I had competed in the same tournament with a rating in the mid USATT 1600s. This year, I was playing there again, only this time within a higher ranked team playing much stronger and more established opponents.

I began the tournament very well. At the end of Friday, my results were very favorable – I closed the day with five wins and one loss. Three of the wins were against USATT 1800 players and the loss was against a USATT 2000 player. In addition to these matches, I was leading two of the matches 2-0 against USATT 1900 players, however my games were spoiled. These matches proceeded as an attempt to save time during the tournament, a usual practice during large events such as the Team Championships. New matches started without waiting for prior matches to be completed and therefore did not count. My teammates closed out their sets, acquiring the necessary points to beat the other team, voiding my anticipated victories.

Friday's last match was one of the best matches I have played. My opponent, a USATT 1800 level player just like myself, took significant leads early several games in a row, only to find me recovering and closing the gap. Then, I continued to press on to win the next few points and securing the games. These comebacks were huge. I was able to recover from being down 7 points to 1 and closing out the game in a deuce, coming back from a 4 point deficit to win the game at 11-8, and finally, being down 4-7 to win the fifth game at 11-8.

This match felt like the match of the century. I was happy and smiling. Gerald stood over by the court barriers and watched. After the match, he said: "Good job. But did you have to make it this dramatic?" I smiled. We both knew that it was a well played match in all of its aspects – mental game, technical game, and physical game. My opponent was very experienced, and fast to boot. He possessed excellent flat hit strokes which were directed to the corners of the table, forcing me to cover a lot of ground in order to return the shots. Nevertheless, time after time I was able to run the ball down, spin it back on the table, and get ready for the next shot.

Saturday, my performance dropped. The tiredness of the previous day showed its ugly face. I fought so hard on Friday to win my matches and allow our team to advance up that I wasted all of the energy that I clearly needed to play well the following day. In some aspects it paid off, as our team advanced one division up - which meant much tougher matches to come against teams consisting of higher rated players.

I did not play well at all in the morning. I was too slow, my reaction time significantly increased. My focus in the game was off and, overall, my mobility was sporadic. I ended the day with three wins and four losses. I did not participate in the last match against another team – I went back to the hotel room to get much needed rest. There was still one more tournament day ahead with many more matches that needed to be played. This was a very good plan – the needed rest paid its dividends.

On Sunday, I closed the day at 2-2 by beating two more USATT 1800 level players and losing to one USATT 1800 and one USATT 1900 level players. I played well against both of these players and was very close to winning. Unfortunately, I wanted to win so badly that I began playing too safe – allowing them to come back and secure victory. Yet, even with these loses, my overall performance was positive. I beat every player with a lower rating than my own. I only lost a single match that went five games, showing a significant improvement in fortitude – Gerald's favorite word of fighting spirit. I also dominated matches outright against many other players if their styles were close to the ones I was familiar with, meaning that my experience and overall strategy has improved significantly.

Back to training

The Team Championships allowed me to see many improvements in my game, but yet again, I had very little interest in the things I did well. I was more concerned with the skills I needed to perfect.

Since Gerald was part of another team and playing his matches during the Team Championships, it was up to me to carefully analyze my game in order to develop a new training plan. I found two specific areas that needed improvement: short game, such as service return, especially the ability to initiate a strong opening on even a short ball. My lack of touch and placement on service returns allowed my opponents to start a strong attack and win the point. Meanwhile, when I was attacked, I lacked speed in my footwork – specifically when I was forced to move to the middle of the table and then attacked wide. In addition, my backhand defense was predictable as I returned the shots to the exact same spot where my opponent initiated his attack, in essence daring my opponent to make the same shot again without needing to use their footwork. This was a no brainer for many advanced players. Not only did they execute this shot flawlessly but it also came with a lot more pace and power. I usually lost such a point.

Gerald and I continued to practice and develop my footwork. With the help of my teammate, Mika, I learned of a couple footwork drills presented by Brian Pace in his videos. I immediately wanted to incorporate these drills into my training. In the very next lesson, Gerald and I began to work using the patterns demonstrated by Brian Pace. I was surprised to find that only a few days of training improved my footwork on the forehand significantly. I learned to remain on the offensive delivering my shots even when they were sent wide to my forehand or straight into my middle. We also began to incorporate elements of the backhand into this drill in order for the backhand to be engaged during training so that I would be ready to execute a backhand shot when the time came.

My next two tournament results were quite modest. I still remained a few points away from USATT 1900. The only noteworthy accomplishment was a good performance against defensive players. I won all matches against defensive players while other players in my event group struggled against the same kind of opponents. This was a true time proven test of the Gerald's "base" system – teaching me the proper means to attack an underspin ball from the very early stages of my development. The skills I had mastered in the early stages of training stayed with me and really differentiated me from my peers against defensive players.

Without further ado, Gerald and I proceeded to work on the next element of the game – improving backhand block and learning to punch through a loop with a backhand. The training was broken up into several phases. The first phase was aimed at developing a consistent block of a strong, spiny loop. This helped me become accustomed to timing the ball correctly as it traveled into my backhand. We then increased the level of difficulty by introducing the punch into the mix. Exercising the punch separately and then mixing it up with blocks became a usual routine. We also touched up on 4th ball attack – where Gerald executed a 3rd ball attack with a strong spiny loop for me to punch the ball with my backhand or block it.

Finally, it came time to play in yet another event.

Breaking USATT 1900

This tournament was just like any other tournament – a usual venue held by the Westfield club in New Jersey. I liked to compete in this club because the club is home to the best players in the country and also serves as one of the main coaching centers in the area. I was eager to gain the next few points to pass the USATT 1900 mark. That was my focus and my training definitely prepared me for it. I signed up to participate in three sections - Under 2000, Under 2200, and the Open.

I quickly advanced into the quarter final in the Under 2000 section by beating my opponents in the group. I was paired against the same USATT 1900 player I had played last time I competed at this venue, who won the match rather easily. The last time we had played, my opponent attacked with every opportunity, while I made many mistakes in my opening, missing my shots and not being able to apply pressure in the game. This time around, the game was different. I was able to keep up with my opponent and freely entered numerous rallies. While I did not win the match, I performed significantly better than I had the first time we were paired. Only a month previously I had lost the match 3-0, with very low scores. This time, I lost with 3 games to 1, losing one game due to a poor service at a 9-10 deficit. This was a good indication of my improvement, and even though I was shut out of the Under 2000 section, I was ready to compete in the other sections.

I won two of my matches in the round robin of the Under 2200 section and was paired against a high USATT 2000 player for the final match that would determine whether I was to advance out of the group. After a short warm up, we began to play. My opponent had a strange game. He had an excellent forehand and slow, spiny unorthodox backhand. His serves were quite tricky. It took me a few shots to get used to his attacks as the placement on his opening shots was very wide. While I struggled during his service, I was able to win both points on my serve and stay even until I finally began to attack his serves and scoring points on his serve as well as on mine. He tried countering my shots close to the table, fighting to control the distance where he had wide angle advantage, but my responses were quick and strong forcing him to retrieve. I won the first game 11-9. In the second game, my opponent decided to stand back and use his retrieving and chopping skills. He was expecting me to miss, but I attacked stronger and stronger. I won this game 11-9 as well. The next game, my opponent was using the same strategy – trying to force me to miss by chopping and retrieving. His expected to wear me out, waiting for me to start making more mistakes. With the games being close, it was a reasonable expectation. Two missed shots would have reversed the game to his favor. Yet, this never happened – I won the next game with a score of 11-8. My opponent congratulated me with a solid handshake and said I played very well. Now, I was happy.

In the next match, I beat a tough USATT 1700 level short pip penhold blocker. My opponent was a good blocker, but he was also capable of attacking a loose ball every now and then with a very fast hit. This element of my opponent's game required me to continue applying pressure on him or either start getting ready for defeat. I lost the first game and won the second. I tried to force my game too soon in the third game and lost at 11-6. Fighting back in the fourth game, I kept my two points advantage throughout the game and evened the match out at 2-2. Unfortunately, I quickly lost two points in the following game on my opponent's serve. Instead of waiting for me to attack, he got his 3rd ball attack ready and swung at the ball first. The combinations followed and the game became very favorable for my opponent – "6 to 2!" he called out.

I took a step back from the table and asked for a timeout. I picked up my towel and wiped the sweat off my forehead. My opponent built a great momentum to close out the match. I needed to recover. Gerald was looking at me ready to offer strategic advice. I looked at him and said: "Gerald, I got it. I am just a bit tired. I know what to do". He nodded in agreement.

As if my towel gave me some magical strength, I began to score points in rapid succession. 2-6 became 4-6. Then, 7-5, 7-7, and on to 8-8. At that point, I had to focus carefully - I had no luxury to repeat the start of the match by being too lenient to initiate an attack on my opponent's serve. I had to make an effort to start with a strong attack on a long serve and keep attacking, but this time, aiming to produce slow loops with strong spin and unpredictable placement. Again, I hesitated to initiate the attack, proceeding to push the serve instead. The ball went a bit too long and my opponent smacked it hard toward my backhand. With no time to react, I punched the air and felt my paddle making contact with the ball. The ball rebounded quickly down the line – right past my opponent's forehand. "Wow, I made it!" I thought to myself. "OK, more confidence, keep swinging" was my next thought as I got back into a ready position. The next point was a long rally, which I won when my opponent missed a block and sent the ball into the net. With two more points to go on my serve, I had an advantage. I played well, looping the ball over and over until my opponent made a fatal mistake. I pulled out yet another win.

Later on, my opponent admitted to having had a high USATT 1900 rating just a few months back, which could explain his confident play against me. I won by only a few close rally points, but I won!

I was excited to pull off another win. In my mind, the prior two wins were sufficient to break USATT 1900 level after the update of the tournament in the following two weeks. I was wondering where I would end up, but ultimately, I had achieved the goal I had set out to reach during this tournament.

Waiting for the next game, I was thinking whether or not I was capable of winning the first place of Under 2200 section. I saw the pairings – the top seed was rated in the mid 2150s. He was likely to win the section even if I made it to the final. I was resting when someone tapped me on the shoulder. This same 2150 player came up to me and said: "We are playing next." I looked at the score sheet with confusion and noticed that the Open section games had begun and that my match against the 2150 player was part of the round robin in the Open section.

I picked up my paddle and went forward. I figured it was good to play against this player in the Open. This way, I would be in a better position to face him in the Under 2200 section.

During the first game, I scored an early four point lead and, to my opponent's dismay, won the game 11-7. Game two saw the scores completely reversed, I lost 7-11. However, this is where things got very interesting. We began to play point for point, scoring points one after another in sequence. We entered rallies full of quick exchanges and we used serves to set up powerful attacks. Both of us hit the ball hard and placed it well. Finally, we reached a crucial point of our stalemate – deuce. I had to play aggressively, but not risky. I went back to basics. I served a short underspin ball to the forehand of my left handed opponent. He pushed the ball, but it trailed too long and I was able to attack the ball with strong spin aiming into his forehand. My opponent tried to blocking the ball, but missed. I won the point. This immediately put pressure on my rival. I eased into the ready position to prepare for the next point.

> *"When your opponent gets nervous, be ready for a long serve as it is much harder to keep it short during mental distress."*

Suddenly, I recalled the last article I read some time ago: "When your opponent gets nervous, be ready for a long serve as it is much harder to keep it short during mental distress." I got ready for anything. The article was correct – the ball traveled slightly longer than usual. I took a swing and looped the ball hard. I won the game with a score of 12-10.

I headed toward Gerald, got a drink and toweled off. "You have a chance to beat him. You must beat him!" I said to myself.

My opponent was in even more trouble as I gained a two points advantage early in the next game. We again began to exchange points until the score reached 8-6 in my favor. My opponent called for a timeout. Gerald gave me instructions and I carefully listened. It was crucial for me to continue being on the offensive. My opponent needed to know that I was ready and capable of winning the point on any weak shot. To beat me, he needed to play higher level of table tennis than I was able to handle.

The timeout ended and I walked back to the table. It was my turn to serve. I repeated the same play that bothered my opponent. I served short to the forehand, my opponent pushed long, and I opened hard to his forehand. The point was won! I was ready to repeat the same sequence, only this time, I paused for a second looking for any signs of movement from my opponent. I was looking for a hint on the best spot I could aim the ball, but I was too late. I missed the ball completely. Wow, I had missed my chance, a very easy ball, but I was still leading 9-7!

All of a sudden my opponent delivered a new serve! It was very different from all other serves he had tried, and it allowed him to win the next two points! "That's OK", I thought, it is now my turn. On my next serve, my attack got blocked strong and wide to my forehand. I rushed to reach it, but I was way too late. I lost the point. My only chance was to win the next point for a yet another Deuce. I relaxed, breathed out and served again. We played a long rally, where I kept on swinging. At some point, my shots were almost instinctive – I simply reacted to the ball, without thinking, using pure animal instinct – and I scored.

We were again in a deuce. The only difference is that my opponent was still using his new serve, but I had the lead and therefore lots of pressure on my adversary! The deuce was ugly. My opponent kept executing his tricky serve and making me miss the ball early, while I had to focus and fight to bring the game back into a deuce.

At 11-11, I again missed the serve. My opponent took the advantage. I served but the ball floated too far and I immediately received a loop. I blocked the ball back, but my opponent redirected the shot deep into the backhand. I ran down and fished the ball up as high as I could in order to bring the ball back on the table. I knew that it was the only chance I had to try and win the point back. The ball bounced high and deep. My opponent's eyes lit up, he swung back and hit the ball as hard as he could. I saw his stroke as if in slow motion – a frame by frame drama unfolded before me as I helplessly watched the ball fly towards me. Milliseconds into the flight of the ball I saw a much different picture than I had anticipated. The ball flew down directly in the net. From the sidelines I heard Gerald's excited voice: "Way to keep the point alive, keep it up!"

> *"The rule of thumb is that better players have the upper hand when games end up in a deuce. Better players have better consistency. The longer the match goes on, the higher is the chance of better players scoring their shots than missing."*

I knew my opponent would serve the same difficult serve again. I got ready to return it. I knew if I tried too hard to attack it I would make a mistake and again be at a disadvantage. Instead of attacking the serve, I tried to return it back on the other side of the table as best I could, hoping to win the point in the rally. It was a better option than giving my opponent a free point by missing a service return. That is exactly what happened. A serve was very spiny yet again. I pushed the serve, guessing the amount of spin on the ball – which was significantly more than I had anticipated. The ball popped up high again. My opponent went for his 3rd ball attack. I again was helpless – quickly retrieving back with thoughts of saving the point with any kind of lob. But to my delight this ball met the same fate as the previous one – my opponent rushed to attack it, sending it into the net.

This was probably the only opportunity for me to win the match. All I needed was one point. The rule of thumb is that better players have the upper hand when games end up in a deuce. It is simply a matter of consistency. Better players have better consistency. The longer the match goes on, the higher is the chance of better players scoring their shots than missing. I needed to make this point count by keeping my play simple. I decided to use the same play that had allowed me to score my points throughout the match.

I served a short underspin serve to my opponent's forehand and as I had planned, received a slightly longer push back as the return of service. I reached back, lowered my knees and exploded with a forehand loop. The response was a quick block right into my middle. I almost fell over rotating my body out of the way in order to make the next forehand shot. The incoming shot was not strong, but the placement was excellent. I lost my balance. My opponent blocked the ball deep into my backhand. The shot was not a slow one, but I clearly remember the words in my head: "Go for it!"

I reached back with my backhand, slightly rotating my body to the left, and exploded forward. I felt the pressure of the ball as if it was sticking to the paddle. Fraction of the second later I saw the ball propel forward, barely clearing the net. This was a perfect execution of one of the shots Gerald and I had worked on when we last strengthened my backhand. The ball hit the table exploding with strong spin, bounced, hit the edge of my adversary's paddle and flew into the ceiling.

The game was over! I've beaten a USATT 2100 level player! I definitely broke USATT 1900!

What I did not yet know was that in this very moment I had finally achieved my ultimate goal - reaching the magical and sought-after rating of USATT 2000.

The tournament was not yet over. Unfortunately the mental and physical energy that I needed to win the previous matches completely drained me. I played my next match against a very consistent USATT 1750 modern defender and struggled. I had little power to drive the ball and felt completely exhausted. I won another game to take the lead of the match, winning 2 games to 1. I came up to towel off before playing the next game and told Gerald: "I have no more strength left to play other matches." He looked at me and said "I agree, I think you have proven yourself and achieved a lot in one day." With these thoughts I won my last match of the day by beating the defender at 3-1.

I had played 9 matches already and still was scheduled to play more by advancing in the Under 2200 section. In addition, one more match was left to play in the Open section. I breathed in a little disappointed to have to give up now - there were only high level players left to play against in the rest of my matches, but I had no choice. I threw in the towel knowing that the days when I was able to compete in 3 to 4 different sections at the same time during the tournament were over. From now on, the games would be a lot tougher and much more physically demanding.

USATT 2000

You may ask why I did not choose to entitle the previous section "Breaking USATT 2000". The answer is quite simple: I did not plan on, nor was intending to break the final barrier and achieve my ultimate goal during that tournament.

I was aiming to achieve a more attainable goal, but my performance turned out to be much better than expected. I had just entered the new level and I could not justify myself to be a solid USATT 2000 player. I had not competed against enough players in this rating range to remain at this level. Teachers always say that it is easier to acquire one "A" in school than to keep one throughout the year. I completely agree with this logic and only time will tell what the future holds.

Meanwhile, I achieved the goal I had set for myself: reaching USATT 2000. This was the result of lots of learning, lots of training, and lots of hard work.

My thoughts and experiences

I hope that my story helped explain the difficult endeavor I have embarked on by the moment I set my table tennis goal. I described my experiences as they occurred during my training and tournament play; however, there are many gaps in my narrative. It would have been an impossible task to document two years and four months of training and competition in further detail. Hence, I turn the page to the second half of my book.

The phrase "a game within the game" perfectly describes the contents of the next section. I have written a set of articles to describe various elements of the game and my thoughts regarding many challenges that a player may face in the course of their table tennis development. I struggled with many of the very elements of table tennis game I describe in the following pages. If I had known or was able to access all the information explained below with ease, my progress would have been much smoother and easer. I strongly believe the material below would be beneficial to break plateaus and shine a light on your continuous improvement.

Learning to play table tennis, I have had many moments described as "Aha Moments" – moments of sudden breakthrough in understanding. During performance slumps or lapses in training, these moments turned the tide quickly, allowing me to recover the initial momentum of improvement, helping me return back on track to achieving my goals.

I certainly hope that the material below will help you experience your own "Aha Moments" and help you improve.

Service practice

Many table tennis players are familiar with the importance of service and service return skills. This is emphasized in almost every table tennis article or book I have ever laid eyes on. The reason is quite simple. Serving well may yield to immediate leads and apply a significant amount of pressure on the opponent. Returning serves efficiently has the same effect – it stops the opponent from being able to initiate their own attack and hence takes away their initiative. This also frequently increases the pressure on the opponent, forcing the opponent to attempt stronger serves - leading to poor serves and free points.

> *"...a common pitfall in a player's development is putting too much emphasis on service practice, too much emphasis on learning how to serve an ace."*

This information is widely known and understood within a table tennis community. Yet, there is an untold part to this story that is rarely discussed in the books or on the court. When must one focus on improving serves? How often? And what kind of serves must one use and work on in order to be more effective?

These questions are rarely asked at the right time, if at all. A lot of time is wasted on developing a strong service prematurely. Quick results against the peers are achieved almost immediately with the better serve, but the improvement stagnates further down the road. Lots of time may go by, addressing many areas of the player's game in order to realize why the player is struggling and not improving. It becomes an even bigger surprise to the player when it is realized that the sole element causing the halt in further improvement is the service, simply because it was improperly introduced into the player's arsenal.

I will not argue the importance of service practice. Service practice has its importance. However, the common pitfall in a player's development is putting too much emphasis on service practice, too much emphasis on learning how to serve an ace. I can imagine the reader's surprised at this statement – how can it be so? This could be somewhat counter intuitive. Nevertheless, let's first take a look at the purpose of the serve.

Service is the only time during table tennis point when the servicing player has a clear advantage over the opponent. Service can be applied with various amounts and types of spin and placement. Service can vary in speed and the speed of service execution. Thus, service is focused on translating the initial advantage into an absolute advantage whether winning the point with a first attack opportunity or gaining a tactical advantage in a combination of shots.

When a player works on improving his serve, quick improvement is visible due to many "easy" points that can be won outright with a great serve. This is even more evident in the beginner and intermediate levels. This advantage gives the player an immediate boost in the game, allowing him to beat many players around the same skill level with ease. Beating the peers, a player advances higher in skill level, however, the service itself will no longer be enough. Better, more experienced opponents know how to return serves well. In the meantime, used to serving aces against his peers, the improved player is expecting the same results from better opponents as well - poor return of a serve, which detrimentally affects other parts of the game. First to suffer is anticipation, footwork, and the consistency of 3rd ball attacks.

When I broke USATT 1600 for the first time, I began to work on my serves. I was able to work on this skill on my own simply using a box with table tennis balls – handy practice for anyone with access to a table. It took a while to learn how to apply spin to the ball, how to vary the spin, how to control the speed and placement of the service. These skills helped developing improved touch and were invaluable to improving service return, yet when I got used to winning serves outright, I experienced instability in my opening shots and rallying skills. In addition, the control over the length of the serve took even longer to master which made serves vulnerable to crushing attacks by stronger players.

With serves consisting primarily in spin variation and placement, but going long, the serves in my games were easily returned by better players. When I served and could not acquire an immediate advantage, I tried to deliver an even stronger serve, frequently resulting in unforced service errors.

I struggled with this for a few months, simply shrugging the issue off because I felt that my opponents were much better than I. When I finally brought it up to Gerald, he came up with an answer to correcting my problem. His recommendation (on this and every other aspect of my game) deserves a lot of recognition. Gerald noted that I was attempting to win the point off my serve immediately and said: "Stop attempting to serve aces. Build your game around your strengths." In order to do so, my focus was to be set on creating several opening patterns that I could alternate. These patterns did not consist of strong services. Instead, they were to be simple but short serves that forced my opponents to return the ball in such a way that I was able to start an attack.

Short serves are not attacked by opponents until they reach around the USATT 1800 level rating, and even then, offensive flips and flicks are not used frequently. Flicks and flips at this level are still considered high risk shots. Therefore, it is better to develop an improved 3rd ball attack following a short serve. Obviously, serves should also alternate the amount of spin and placement in order to be even more effective.

The result of the tweaking the strategy of my service delivery was incredible. My opening attacks became stronger due to my training focused on delivering a vicious 3rd ball attack. With immediate pressure of my consistent 3rd ball attack, my opponents began to miss the return of my very simple serves. Meanwhile, my serves were not becoming stronger. They remained the same, short and consistent. The reason for winning serves immediately was the pressure applied by my consistent opening shots. My opponents needed to do more to the ball in order to

www.breaking2000.com

avoid my opening shot. It was not enough to simply return the ball, the opponents needed to return the serves either offensively or succeed in placing the ball where my opening shot was not strong and consistent.

Let's now take a look at long serves. Long serves have an opposite effect to short serve responses leading to immediate rallying. They invite the opponent to commence an attack. If the serves trail long, a player must be able to recognize this serve and prepare for rallying in order to win the point. Expanding the training to recognize long serves and preparing for rallying is also necessary. However, this again becomes more important at higher levels. In the lower and intermediate levels of table tennis, the main response to a serve is still a push.

Thus, first focus on developing strong opening shots against a variety of service returns. This will provide the proper foundation for future development of the skills. Practice serves gradually aiming at building a solid understanding of spin. Be sure to integrate the service and its delivery with the rest of your game by practicing serve and attack. And remember, in the early stages of development of your game, in Gerald's words: "Do not aim to win aces."

Practicing against junk rubber players

I recall practicing with Gerald in one of the local YMCA recreational rooms. The room was secluded and allowed us to train without distractions. Seeking for opponents to play, one of the better players of the club popped into the room. He watched me for a minute, where I was looping the ball many times in a row against a pip block. When I missed the ball and walked over the pick it up, he asked with a smirk: "Why are you wasting your time on training against pips? It will not improve your game. It is a waste of time." I trusted my coach in knowing which skills I had to work on and when, and therefore simply ignored the comment. However, the lack of practice against pips is a very frequently overlooked skill. With fewer and fewer players using defensive alternate equipment coverings due to the new post speed glue era, practicing against players using this equipment is a must for every developing player.

> **"...the lack of practice against pips is a very frequently overlooked skill."**

For me, the training was deemed necessary following my poor match against a long pip blocker in one of the tournaments. The training method proved to be beneficial by the win against the same opponent only one month later. Therefore, we allocated the time to train and to keep refreshing my skills against "junk" rubbers. Many players however do the opposite. They stay away from players using pips and anti coverings. They do this in training and lose easily in tournaments to much lower rated opponents with these styles. Some players stagnate in their development as well. These players win against many players with inverted

www.breaking2000.com

rubbers and raise their rating level only to meet and lose to multiple lower ranked players with such equipment at a later time. This is another form of stagnating progress – all acquired wins are negated by losses against specific styles. These players can be found in many tournaments. They are found complaining about their tricky opponents with pips, long pips, anti, etc.

> *"Wondering what specifically must be worked on during practice with "junk" players? Everything! Every single thing practiced with a partner using an inverted rubber must also be practiced with a player using pips or anti."*

What makes it so difficult to play against players with these styles? In order to understand this, one must learn what kind of effects the above mentioned rubbers have on a ball. I will not focus on explaining the many variations and effects these rubbers have on the ball. It would take a whole book to describe the differences. Perhaps I am exaggerating, however this is exactly why it is important to practice against these styles. If you have a coach or a training partner that does not use these alternate rubber coverings, make friends with any of these players you can find. You will find practice with these players invaluable.

Wondering what specifically must be worked on during practice with "junk" players? Everything! Every single thing practiced with a partner using an inverted rubber must also be practiced with a player using pips or anti. Start with practicing pushes and learn how to keep a push low. Learn the reversal of spin if the opponent's rubber allows it. Make sure to note where the contact of the ball with the table tennis paddle needs to be made. Finally, learn to loop the ball against numerous pip blocks – it will improve your spin game. This type of training will reap significant benefits if practiced regularly.

> **"...junk rubbers are used by most of the players to hide a weakness in their game."**

Lastly, any developing player needs to realize that junk rubbers are used by most of the players to hide a weakness in their game. This could be a lack of footwork, an inability to exchange shots in a fast pace rally, a poor service return using inverter rubber or many other reasons. Once consistent attack against a pip or anti response is developed, which does not have to be very strong, fast and powerful, it will expose the weakness of the "junk" player. Probing different shots and tactics simply by being capable of making the shot over and over would give you the upper edge in your match. You are sure to see more wins on the result sheet – that is a proven certainty.

Gerald once told me: "You must develop an attacking game against "junk" players that is so strong, that meeting players of this style in tournaments will begin to feel like a bye." With Gerald's training, I became known in my local area as a player with an excellent game against defensive players, and even though not every match plays out as a "bye", it is a very empowering feeling when I am able to maintain and take full control in a match against players using alternate rubber coverings and defensive styles.

Facing demons

A developing player who attends different clubs and tournaments will encounter many other players who started their training around the same time as he or she did. Table tennis community is quite small, which means that encountering the same opponents in many different tournaments is a frequent occurrence. If the same opponents are also training, they often improve their game at around the same pace as oneself. Receiving same quality formal training, playing these same opponents over a period of time frequently feels as if one is playing against him or herself. I call these rivals demons.

When I began participating in tournaments frequently, I had to play a lot of matches against players that were improving their game at about the same rate as I. Even now, I know a handful of players that have reached the same level as I have, and some even higher levels. The pitfall of most players when they play their demons is a strong emphasis on previous games – the tactics, services and, most of all, the match result.

It may seem safe to assume that the opponent's game cannot have progressed considerably since the last match. However, this is exactly where the demons get taken for granted. Following the same patterns and expecting to find weakness in the same area of the game could be erroneous and lead to your demise. This is especially true if you secured a victory in your last match against the opponent. If the opponent does not respond with the shots you anticipated based on your last pairing, mistakes can quickly lead to giving up a few points lead. Finally, the mental game of playing a familiar, previously beaten player and struggling during the match often leads to a loss.

> *"Keep paying attention to the player's game and dismiss the previous results achieved against the same player. This will give you a stronger mental game and help you stay focused if the match gets tight."*

How can you successfully beat your demons? The answer is simple: do not assume anything. Treat the game as you would any new game against an unknown opponent and keep probing for weaknesses. Old weaknesses may still exist, or new weaknesses could be discovered where there was no weakness before. Keep paying attention to the player's game and dismiss the previous results achieved against the same player. This will give you a stronger mental game and help you stay focused if the match gets tight.

In order to make the best of your mental strength – reinforce yourself with confidence by

www.breaking2000.com

focusing on the following thoughts: "I am a much better player, I will win." On the other hand, if you are still struggling to beat the demon, try not to get upset. Your opponent may have improved significantly since your last game by practicing a specific area of the game and may now be able to reverse the roles. If you play your game, attack when needed, defend when necessary and continue playing with a fighting spirit and still miss, don't worry about it. This is just a loss and it is not an obstacle as opposed to playing defensively, halting your footwork and blocking easy shots, missing opportunities to attack, and giving up the initiative completely.

I played against numerous demons and I sometimes lost the battle against them myself. I can remember a particular match playing against a demon. I had won the first game, but then I got tight. I completely gave up the initiative and lost. After the game, Gerald came up to me and said: "If you keep taking your shots, eventually…" he paused looking at me as if expecting me to say it. I continued his phrase hesitantly "I will be making them?" He smiled with approval.

No mercy, no hesitation

One can meet a lot of opponents in this game. Some may be your peers. Some are older gentlemen, ladies, kids or Paralympics players. Everyone competes in the same tournaments and if you're not ready to play the match with a solid focus, you will give up the wins needlessly.

I was almost instantly faced with these challenges when I first entered the tournament scene. I was 28 years old and quite athletic. I am not a big guy by all means, however when compared to a 10 or 11 year old kid, I look like a monster – a mean, unshaven, almost angry looking man. I was on the winning side that day because my younger opponent hesitated and feared me. Yet, the next match, the tables turned on me.

> **"Do not look at your opponent as anything other than an opponent – a fierce opponent. Their rating represents their skill, which is what you are here to compete against. Age, style, height, strength – none of these elements are important in this game. Focus on the ball."**

I faced a little boy who must have been no older than 7 or 8 years old. It was comical to look at the other side of the table and to only be able to see his head and the paddle. My perception of my opponent quickly changed after the first few points were played out.

The little guy attacked me hard and strong. If I returned the shot, he smacked the ball even harder to the opposite side of the table. I was in awe – running around the table while the kid had full control. When I tried to find the mental strength to attack, I hesitated. I was afraid of hitting the ball hard. Being a nice guy and a small kid growing up, I remembered being picked on by older boys. I could not activate my killer instinct against my opponent and conceited by never playing the game I had practiced.

This match brought on a more acute realization of the importance of the mental game. Gerald said to me: "Do not look at your opponent as anything other than an opponent – a fierce opponent. Their rating represents their skill, which is what you are here to compete against. Age, style, height, strength – none of these elements are important in this game. Focus on the ball."

> **"Remember, only one player will come out a winner in a match. It is up to you to fight in order to win regardless of who you face."**

Gerald was absolutely correct. This sound advice was again emphasized by another loss. I was rated in the mid USATT 1500 and had to compete against a paralympic player in a wheel chair. My opponent was a number one seed on the table with a rating in the mid USATT 1900s. Earlier, I beat an USATT 1850 player and had given another USATT 1800 player a scare, losing in the 5th game. I seemed to have all the elements to beat my opponent. Yet, when we began our game, I quickly lost. I could not find the strength to attack a player in a wheelchair.

This was yet another revelation. If I was to continue advancing through the ranks and becoming a better player, I needed to play hard all the time without hesitation or mental lapse, regardless of the opponents I faced. It took some time to adjust, but a few months later I played a new junior rising star, easily the most unique girl in the area. At only six years old, she was beating many older and experienced players. My first game against her was a loss, but I recalled Gerald's comments and started the next game with a fresh mindset, closing the match at 3-1. After that day, the girl became my rival. I played against her numerous times and was a witness to her progress, seeing her get past me in rating points. Yet I played her hard and won every time I faced her in a match.

Remember, only one player will come out a winner in a match. It is up to you to fight in order to win regardless of who you face.

Hollywood shots

This is quite a short section, but definitely a section worth writing about. I recall learning the forehand loop and then seeing how I was able to magically bring it into the game. It felt great. My shot was fast and powerful. I became so fascinated with it that I frequently made my shot and then… completely stopped. All of my attention was aimed at observing the ball – watching my shots as if I was watching a Hollywood action blockbuster.

At first, this little weakness of wonder had no adverse side effects. My opponents were not strong enough to return the shot. However, when I advanced to play higher level players this behavior became an immediate problem. I was not prepared to handle even the weakest return of my attacking shot.

The little problem became a huge issue. Not only did I have to learn to stop watching my shots, I had to learn to move and anticipate a response all at the same time. The complexity of mastering this skill became even harder.

Always be ready to move and always be ready for the most unexpected returns of your shots. It will not be possible to return all of the shots – even world class players are unable to do so. However, if each return can be attacked over and over, the initiative will remain, leading to more pressure on your opponent with very favorable chances to win the point.

"First, focus on the development and the consistency training of the offensive weapon.

Then, your focus must be aimed at learning to deal with possible responses to the offensive weapon such as blocks, counter attacks, and available angles."

I recall playing a long pip blocker in a club game. He returned my loops deeply several times throughout the match, hitting the edge of the table. Magically, I was able to loop each and every one of these edge shots back onto the table and win the points.

My opponent was looking at his shots as the "Hollywood shots", and he did not expect me to bring those shots back, but I did.

The best suggestion I can offer to you is to always train using two phases. First, focus on the development and the consistency training of the offensive weapon. This involves training the offensive weapon using a number of shots that are used to set up the offensive weapon. In my case it was a 3rd ball attack that was initiated through a short underspin serve, followed by my opponent's half long or long push. The second phase must be aimed at learning to deal with possible responses to the offensive weapon such as blocks, counter attacks, and available angles. This must be trained in succession after the consistency of the offensive weapon becomes very high.

The aim of this training method is to unite the developing offensive weapon with the rallying skills early in a player's career. This will prepare the player for a solid continuous offensive game a lot sooner and will eliminate some stagnating improvement that is caused by untrained skills of transitioning from delivering an opening attack shot to rallying.

This skill can be easily developed by opening up offensive weapon training to finish off the point as if you were playing a real match. In my case, 3rd ball training was modified to finish the point in a rally after any 3rd ball attack was returned. Thus, becoming 5th ball training.

Focus on the opening attack and be prepared for the next shot at all times. The sooner you become accustomed to being prepared for the next shot, the better you will be prepared for a high level table tennis game. Finally, if you feel that your "Hollywood shots" are very important for you, capture them with a camcorder.

I hate playing him!

If I had received a dime for every time I heard someone utter those words, I would be a very wealthy man. Why do so many developing players feel this way?

I have already mentioned the difficulty some emerging players have in dealing with "junk" players. This section will expand to cover a bigger group of adversaries. While some players in this category might be using alternate rubber coverings on their paddles, they are better identified as players that did not receive any formal coaching; players that developed their own style of the game purely by feel.

These players are frequently referred to as unorthodox because their styles have become influenced by many factors outside of the game of table tennis. A clear example would be a tennis player that transitions over to table tennis. Such a player is fast – he or she has a great consistency and a lot of power on forehand, a somewhat large and strange slice chop on the backhand, but, more importantly, is most vitally known for his or her ability to impart spin the ball. Years of coordination with a bigger, heavier ball allow these players to control a small ball with a magician's uncanny touch.

> *"Due to the lack of formal training, unorthodox players develop their own almost random responses to shots, frequently placing the ball in an area on the table that feels unintuitive to a trained player."*

Why would these opponents cause so much trouble to developing players? While it may seem a difficult question to answer, the answer lies in only one area of the game: anticipation. Due to the lack of formal training, unorthodox players develop their own almost random responses to shots, frequently placing the ball in an area on the table that feels unintuitive to a trained player. In addition, unorthodox players do not evaluate risk when making even the most difficult shots: they are fully relaxed and they just go for it. An example of such risk evaluation is an unorthodox player punching a very low and spiny ball and making the shot every time.

Obviously, developing player who had only played opponents offering a text book response to their shots will find playing an unorthodox player quite challenging. With developing players unable to anticipate the responses and making more mistakes in the process, the game and match will begin to slip away. The loss can come even quicker if the player's mental game starts to deteriorate due to hesitation, rashness, or inaction.

To challenge this pattern and allow the developing player to remain in control, it is important

www.breaking2000.com

to continue to reinforce proper strategy in the early stages, from beginner and intermediate levels. Unorthodox players usually have more weaknesses, but they may not be exposed by inexperienced players. For example, if a player is trying to force unorthodox player to make more errors using stronger serves. Strong serves put unorthodox players under pressure, forcing them to use their best strength to return the shot. In this scenario, stronger serves would not work. Instead, simplicity is most often the key to beating unorthodox opponents. Simple, weaker serves do not seem threatening and will be returned with less force, allowing you to assume full control of the point. In addition, slowing down the game is usually a better option as the slow spiny shots are quite rare for unorthodox players to encounter and need a special feeling of touch in order to deal with them. The main goal is to continue exposing weaknesses and modifying your strategy focusing to always attacking the weakest part of your opponent's game.

I recall playing in a tournament and facing off a very fast and eager gentleman with pips on both sides. I had already begun training against pip players, but I had never seen pips being used in such an aggressive fashion. My opponent sliced the ball sharp left and sharp right, forcing me to move until I had to roll an easier ball on the table just to stay in the point. Every time I did this, and even when I returned the ball low, the ball was smashed in the opposite direction. I did not give up and continued to play my game. The first thing I had to address was the sharp slice – I had to stop using short serves. They were too easily returned, with sharper angles than I have anticipated or they were dropped short. I also served into one side of the table, creating wide angles for my opponent to use.

> *"Challenge yourself to find new weaknesses in unorthodox players whether you have played the opponent in the past or not. This will make your understanding of the game, your mental strength, and your strategy superior, helping you prepare for yet another jump in skill level."*

I made this adjustment and began serving long into the middle of the table, my opponent began to miss even this relatively easy serve. When the service was returned, it was easy for me to attack and win the point. Seemingly a small minor adjustment allowed me to take control of the game and win.

After the match, I was approached by another player who was complaining about playing my opponent earlier and losing to him. My opponent beat a few players around my USATT 1500 rating that day, while truly his skill level was not all that high. Yet, he was able to combine what he knew into a pattern that was not frequently encountered by trained table tennis players and create a point winning combination that eventually won him games and sets.

Instead of saying "I hate to play him," start saying "I would love to beat him." Challenge yourself to find new weaknesses in unorthodox players whether you have played the opponent in the past or not. This will make your understanding of the game, your mental strength, and your strategy superior, helping you prepare for yet another jump in skill level.

Slow spin

During my initial forehand training with Gerald, I swung at the ball with all the force I had as if there was no other way to hit the ball. Power was not an element I had ever lacked. Yet, I felt that if I did not swing at the ball with everything I had, I would not be able to loop.

It took Gerald many months to teach me to relax and control my swing, but this training proved to be well worth it. My rating was around USATT 1300 at the time. I faced a young player in one of the local table tennis tournaments. Immediately, in the first game, it became clear that I could not outplay him using speed. I lost the first game and received coaching advice from Gerald: "Junior players are trained to loop fast and faster. They are not taught to think. Use it – give him a slow loop and always a slow loop."

As minor as this advice seemed to be, it led to great results: I won the next three games with relative ease. For the first time I realized the importance of a slow loop. As I developed my game, there were many moments similar to this one where a slow loop was a more effective shot.

As my skill level increased, my slow loop was refined to be applicable against a wider range of shots such as long pip blocks, short and anti chops, inverted rubber chops, no spin and slow topspin balls. In addition, the loop trajectory changed, sending the ball lower over the net and much closer toward the end line. Finally, the slow loop became my ultimate response to many serves and had a much more serious impact on my game, as it allowed me to set up my power loop. I no longer had to swing hard right away, but instead I could "move" my opponent off balance a bit by the slow loop and attack his next shot with a lot of force.

If you do not lack power in your loops, concentrate on developing a slow, spiny loop. At the higher levels of table tennis, this skill is crucial. Once you think you have mastered this shot, challenge yourself further: use it in a three or four shot combination altering the speed of the loop. Now you have embarked into an even higher level of training: rhythm training.

Be proud, you're doing great!

The winner always wants the ball

In one of my favorite movies, "The Replacements", the coach said these words to his quarterback after a he hesitated during the play and instead of running the ball in for a touch-down, attempted to execute a failed pass. I found this comment to be true in table tennis as well. It deals with the effort needed in order to win the most important points of the game: the so called 11-9s and deuces, the most crucial points required to beat the most persistent peers and higher ranked players.

As I began to play more tournament games, Gerald noticed that I had a tendency to play well even with players many hundred points higher, but that I eventually lost in a close situation with scores of 11-8, 11-9, or in a deuce. It was evident that my mental game was not strong enough to play my best table tennis regardless of the final scores. I made many mistakes under pressure. Even when my consistency began improving in match critical situations, I had trouble closing out the games and winning.

While prior to improving my mental game I was losing my games subconsciously due to complete indecision or due to a lack of proper risk assessment and being overly aggressive, after improving my mental game I began to consciously lose games by giving up the initiative to my opponent on purpose. Giving up the initiative had some good results against my peers since most of my rivals had similar issues attempting to go for the win. Against better players, however, deliberately giving up the initiative amounted to the same as giving up. Better players took the opportunity to win the points outright and at will.

Gerald told to me something that I have carried with me into every match from that day on. "Against better players, you must play your best and you must swing at the ball all the time. You do no need to go crazy trying to kill it, but you must continue working with the ball and instead of throwing it over the net for your opponent to smash. Remember, better players have more experience and better consistency than you.

This means that in the long run, the odds are in their favor. You need to eliminate those odds by winning your points early."

It took me a few months to incorporate this advice into my game. Mental training to consciously deliver desired behavior takes time. It takes even longer for the conscious part of you to transition your reactions into subconscious actions. However, when the moment finally came for my subconscious thoughts to take over, I no longer felt severe pressure in close scores and deuces. I began not only to pull off incredible comebacks, but also to win some important games and matches, described by one table tennis commentator as winning "at the first time of asking."

Rating fluctuations explained

I called this section rating fluctuations because it is a tangible measurement that is available to any table tennis player registered with USATT. If competition in tournaments is a regular affair, a charting feature on the USATT rating page can demonstrate a player's rating change over time.

This is a very valuable feature for any player actively involved in setting goals, measuring the rate of their success, and working on breaking down and analyzing their game. The analysis of the game is performed during usual intervals to set new training goals that need to be established or modified in order to continue improving. Since I was regularly analyzing my game following the tournaments, I was able to notice that I usually lost quite a few tournaments in a row, and hence many rating points right before I broke out and beat a lot of players. I frequently accumulated wins so rapidly after a fluctuation that they compensated for previous losses and lead to the acquisition of enough points to move me a whole level higher.

Initially, I was not very happy to see this fluctuation. I felt that loosing so many points before recovering was detrimental to my game. I would rather gradually keep acquiring small amounts of points. Yet, when I began to ask myself why I was losing and what my training focused on during the period when my rating curve decreased, I started to realize that what was occurring was in fact not a bad phenomenon. It represented a typical learning curve.

To better illustrate this, let's look at two examples of such fluctuations in my game. Both of these fluctuations occurred quite close to each other – one while I was in USATT 1600 and another around USATT 1700 level. Both of these fluctuations occurred for different reasons.

When I broke USATT 1600, Gerald and I began to put more emphasis on consistent attack of a defensive ball. This training was aimed at shaping me into a strong offensive player, able to match up against a wide range of defensive players, mainly choppers and blockers. As a result, my game began to change. Instead of opening my 3rd ball attack with a hard fast loop, I began to loop with heavier spin and at much reduced speed. When this training transitioned into tournament games, the results became clear: I was performing very well against defensive players, but struggled significantly against offensive players. I lost many matches to peers with offensive styles several tournaments in a row.

> *"It became clear to me that the fluctuations in ratings and temporary laps in performance against a specific set of styles is nothing to be upset about. Experiencing losses is never pleasant, but it is not always a sign of failure – in many cases, it is a natural side-effect of improvement!"*

Once Gerald and I reached the desired level of consistency in the attack of the defensive style game, we again returned to the basics – training aimed at re-establishing the consistency of the basic strokes against topspin ball, blocking, service, and service return. We always refreshed these specific skills after learning new material or after working on improving consistency in one specific area of the game.

It took a few weeks to recover the lost consistency of the old shots. Yet, when those skills recovered, they came back with even more strength, leading to incredible results. I was beating many opponents, which most of the time resulted in significant rating level adjustments.

It became clear to me that the fluctuations in ratings and temporary laps in performance against a specific set of styles is nothing to be upset about. Experiencing losses is never pleasant, but it is not always a sign of failure – in many cases, it is a natural side-effect of improvement! Therefore, if you are working on improving one part of your game and you notice that you're having a harder time remaining consistent in the areas of the game which used to be your strengths, do not be alarmed. Do not turn back! Keep improving the new area of the game until you reach the desired results. Then, come back to recover prior strengths and you will see immediate results.

In order not to lose the quality of the newly learned material, try to bring the new training elements into the refresher training aimed at rebuilding the consistency of your prior strengths. For example, if you began working on a push and your forehand loop against topspin suffered as a result of this training, try to start your drill with a few pushes before converting the game into a topspin to topspin forehand looping. This will strengthen both areas of your game and bring them together into a nice, solid combination.

Another fluctuation occurred when Gerald and I began to develop my backhand as an offensive weapon. This fluctuation took place several times for the exact same reason. It involved changes of the backhand attacking shot as Gerald and I were working on a backhand punch, then backhand loop, then backhand slow spin. Backhand training was a lot more difficult and wide focused. It greatly affected my forehand footwork patterns and anticipation as I began to prefer to use my backhand against certain shots on which I used to use a forehand. The fluctuations were numerous – some were more significant than others, yet in the long run, all of the lost "territory" was recovered again after some reinforcement of the basics.

Some players become puzzled when they learn new material and find themselves losing to the players they always used to beat. If this happens to you, do not dwell on it. Be aware of what you are improving in your game. Do not deviate from your training plan until you achieve the desired strength and consistency in performing the new skill. Then go back to basics to polish up any skills that have been neglected for a little while. You will find yourself beating these players a lot easier this time around.

Patience is the key to quick and sound improvement. Trust me!

Wide range of practice partners

I already discussed the importance of training against players using pips or anti rubber covering. This section expands on that subject to cover training against players of all other styles.

I have always attended many different table tennis clubs in my area, which enabled me to play against opponents with different styles quite frequently. Most players I know have been looking for training partners with certain styles but have been unable to find them. While there are a lot of table tennis players, styles are quite diverse and it is safe to assume that there are as many different table tennis styles as there are players. So let's take a look at what makes up a table tennis style.

Style in table tennis goes beyond the technique that is used to execute a stroke. Style goes deeper into footwork patterns, preferences for backhand versus forehand, shot selection, preferences whether to attack the ball hard or soft. Every reaction to an incoming ball or every combination of shots coming from the player is an element of style. Style is a way a player links the shots into combinations. All of the shots and combinations are influenced by the player's stroke technique. In short, style is simply the specific way any given player plays the game.

Obviously, since every player plays the game differently, it is easy to recognize certain styles that are problematic for a player. One sure sign is the loss of a game or a match. Other visible signs of style struggle are a noticeable lack of initiative when playing against certain opponents and the inability to properly anticipate the opponent's responses.

I recall having trouble playing one particular opponent and losing to him easily quite frequently. By persistently continuing to play him, I recognized that I was losing simply because I was not used to playing against an opponent who controlled angles the way he was. In addition to controlling angles and attacking wide on both sides, he delivered flat shots that were very fast and powerful, but with little to no spin. It was difficult for me to win against this player, and even though I came close to beating him a few times, I still was unable to overcome his stronger shots. I needed to work against similar shots as my opponent was producing in a training environment and figure out how to win.

I turned to Gerald for help. He watched me play this troublesome opponent and came up with a few practice routines that I could work on during our training sessions. Several weeks later, I walked away from the table against my rival with a win. I was able to defend against and successfully counter the incoming shots comfortably.

> *"A developing table tennis player needs to play many different players not only to develop the antidotes to other player's styles, but also to adopt improved shots and techniques that may be superior to those he or she already possesses."*

This is only one of many examples that demonstrate how recognizing strengths and weaknesses in the game can lead to faster improvement. One fact is certain, had I not played this opponent over and over and lost, I would have had to go through this experience anyways, only probably in a less favorable situation. Only by frequently attending a wide range of clubs in the area, I was able to encounter a player with such a style, identify new weaknesses in my game and rectify them.

I recommend attending as many clubs and tournaments as possible. Too many players are attached to their local clubs. If your table tennis club has a small membership base, the development of your skills will stagnate. A developing table tennis player needs to play many different players not only to develop the antidotes to other player's styles, but also

www.breaking2000.com

to adopt improved shots and techniques that may be superior to those he or she already possesses. The aim is to pick up sufficient experience so that there are no obvious performance gaps when faced to compete against players with familiar and unfamiliar opponents alike.

In the meantime, if you come across a new player who has something unique about his game – something that you have not yet seen, try to train or play against this player every chance you get. This will raise your awareness of newly encountered shots and may also teach you to develop proper anticipation and response to these shots and similar shots as well.

Equipment

There are many different types of equipment available to table tennis players. It goes without saying that it would be unreasonable to expect each player to try every blade and rubber combination in order to find the best suitable too for his or her game. Despite this, many players fall into the habit of constantly searching for an ideal weapon, completely changing their focus from developing an improved technique or learning a new skill. The quest dangerously guides the player to become a table tennis material research scientist.

> *"...experiments [with equipment] have been great at teaching me more __about__ the different materials available, rather than how to better use this equipment in a match.*
>
> *Game wise, I found that I still played best using the same old five ply wooden blade with a somewhat faster rubber capable of generating excellent spin."*

I am certain that I am not the first player to mention equipment and the dangers of experimenting with different equipment for too long and too often. I have found myself experimenting with equipment too much at some point. I recall switching from fast equipment to slow, altering different blades with different handles, switching between blades with different properties – hard, soft, and composite. In the long run, these experiments have been great at teaching me more about the different materials available, rather than how to better use this equipment in a match. Game wise, I found that I still played best using the same old five ply wooden blade with a somewhat faster rubber capable of generating excellent spin.

> *"The most important thing I have discovered while sticking to the same equipment is in learning how to use my technique to vary the types of shots I was attempting to produce."*

The equipment I use now is slightly better than the equipment I used when I began playing the game. However, the experience in reaching the point where I no longer considered equipment as the main source of my development and the main source of my problems on the court has been invaluable. Consciously, I made a decision to stop experimenting with equipment for several months and noticed as a result that my game kept improving even when I felt that I needed a different rubber or blade in order to make better shots. Sticking with the same equipment, I also noticed that there was a lot more potential in my equipment than I had ever dared to explore.

The most important thing I have discovered while sticking to the same equipment is in learning how to use my technique to vary the types of shots I was attempting to produce. For example, my current blade is quite soft and flexible, making smashing and flat hitting a difficult task requiring proper contact. I had to practice hard to understand how to apply these shots using my equipment. Of course it would have been easier to use a harder, stiffer blade, but then my looping would have needed adjustment. I chose to keep my looping skills intact and learn how to use the same material to produce a wider array of shots. I took the right path and this path paid off in due time. No type of blade will ever allow you to immediately excel in every shot. Pick the material that you are most comfortable with, which will require *some* experimentation, and then learn to perfect your game around your chosen tools.

To this day, I see players change their equipment because they like the name of the blade or admire the professional player who uses it. I see the players trying to desperately keep up with the latest and the greatest rubbers the industry can produce. Yet these players seem to remain in the same skill level without much improvement.

To reach USATT 2000, it is not necessary to use the best blades and rubbers. The equipment does not win the games on its own. Games are won by players who work on their skills and learn to apply them on the table using whatever equipment that suits their style, equipment that is comfortable, and easy to control.

If you find yourself playing with a wide variety of equipment, pick the one you like the best and put the rest in a box for 6 months. Challenge yourself not to open this box until at least 6 months have passed. Finally, work on developing your skills with our chosen tool within this time frame. If you have the discipline to practice hard and not open the box, you will see a clear difference in your game, and will eventually find that you have no desire to go rummaging for different tools.

Dealing with mental tactics

I wish I could say that learning table tennis is fun and easy all the time. Unfortunately, this would have been a lie. This game is not only difficult to learn and to play, but it also demands high level of mental skills and toughness. This is true in tournament setting as well as in a club match.

One of the most gruesome and difficult things to deal with in this game is other players – players that do not want to give up their reputation by losing to another, especially lower level player. Frequently, these players use trickery and mental tactics in order to defeat technically superior developing players. Such tactics vary from an opponent slowing down the game and pacing himself to fetch the ball, taking too long to get settled into a ready position, serving too quickly and not waiting for their opponent to settle, making a lot of noise, or any other distracting tactics they can think of. In club play, one can also encounter illegal serves and calling lets on good services.

All of these elements can be a distraction and adversely impact the game. With a game being already too short and fast, there is no time for distraction or hesitation. A developing player must learn to deal with these "curveballs" when they come up.

It would be easy for me to say that anyone can deal with this without much difficulty. Yet that is not always the case. Some players are simply not mentally tough enough to continue playing the best table tennis they can play when the opponent "gets into their head." There are, however, some strategies that can be used to minimize the impact of such tactics.

First and foremost, a developing player must learn the rules of the game. It is interesting to find that many players are still unfamiliar with all areas of the table tennis rule book. Service rules remain one of the primary rules that need to be clearly understood. Toweling off rule, timeout rule, etc are good to know as well.

Secondly, if your opponent constantly uses rushed timing tactics when getting ready for a point, take control of the ball until *you* are ready to play the point. If the ball is in your hand, as when you are getting ready for a service return, the ball will not be served until you pass it over to your opponent. Choose your own pace of the match instead of responding to your opponents. If the ball is in your opponent's hands, make sure to raise your hand up in the air to indicate lack of readiness until ready position is reached. This will prevent the opponent from rushing the serve and catching you unprepared for return.

Finally, if the opponent is taking their time attempting to make you anxious, use the time to relax and think about the previous point and the next point instead. This delay may seem disruptive at first, yet it gives you valuable time to win the next point in your head before it is even played out on the court. Think about strategy adjustments – whether they need to be made, ask yourself about your opponent's weaknesses, ask yourself whether your opponent has any tendencies that would allow you to target them with tactical combination play. Being able to focus on your match will reinforce your game and will build proper thinking even for the games when the opponent is not stalling on purpose.

To deal with loud opponents, one of two things can be done. One solution is to cheer your own good points. This reinforces your mental game and counters the opponent's cheer. While this is a good advice, try not to turn the game into a screaming competition. Another solution is to remain calm and to play your match quietly, even when the opponent cheers their winning points loudly. If the above mentioned does not work, there is another incentive. I assure you that as long as you score your points, your opponent will remain quiet. You have complete control to quiet them down - make your shots!

Pick the response that suits your game and personality and allows you to play your match without distraction. Your natural reaction is usually the one that will achieve better results. Learn what works best for you to be a mentally strong player.

Remember, regardless of distractions and the mental tactics your opponent may attempt to force on you, always retain your cool and a clear, pure line of thought. The opponents utilizing these mental tactics are relying on you to become distraught, impatient, and frustrated. Instead, show them no sign of weakness and play your game with unaffected confidence.

This last advice serves as a good counter tactic. Remember that players who try to intimidate you with these tricks often lack confidence in their own skill and ability to defeat you. Keep this in mind and turn the situation to your advantage. Once the opponent realizes that nothing is working, you will be in full control of their mental state and hence, of the match.

Training and tournament play

When I was just starting out playing the game, I remember being impressed watching two particular players practice. They would first hit the ball back and forth with great speed, then these players backed off the table and counter looped. Finally, after some repetition, these players began to alternate chopping and looping to each other. The training looked very professional as both of the players were focused on repeating their shots with good precision and consistency.

As I improved, I noticed that these two players religiously went through this training routine for about an hour or two prior to their club matches. Unaltered, this routine was solidly engraved into the fundamentals of their game. Yet, what I noticed above all was that while these players trained consistently, their skills did not seem to improve radically. They were certainly getting better practicing against each other, but in the tournaments, their games did not show any significant improvement. The monster shots they used in training never came up in tournament play.

Over time, I came to realize why my game was developing further at a faster rate: Gerald and I constantly changed our training to focus on a different goal. If we worked on a specific skill longer than on others, it was done in order to improve the consistency of that particular skill and make it a high percentage weapon. Any other time, our training was constantly evolving to address one very important table tennis element: change.

> **"...the same practice cannot yield different results."**

Comparing my training with that of the players I have described above, I began to see where their training lacked. Not only were they simply repeating their shots in an unrealistic match scenario, they were practicing shots outside of their styles. For example, they chopped to each other to allow the partner to attack a chop as part of the training, even though the chop was neither player's main stroke. It was never intended to be a weapon used in a real match, however in a tournament setting the chop came out quite frequently as a response to a strong loop. It became obvious that under pressure, a chop became a comfortable and familiar response to an incoming ball, even though it was an incorrect response for an attacking player. The "comfortable" chop came as both the elements of the footwork in training and the anticipation of the incoming ball were repeated numerous times during practice, making this shot a subconscious response.

This observation brings about the old saying regarding practice: "Practice does *not* make perfect. *Proper* practice makes perfect." Comparing this with the two players I have described, it is interesting to point out that the same practice cannot yield different results. These talented players became a victim of their own routine by repeating what they did well and not addressing skills they did not do well.

Today, I am a lot more experienced in table tennis, both in respect to playing and training. I have come to recognize the need to alter my training and to set specific training goals for each exercise. It is not enough to assume that in order for someone to improve, one simply needs to practice, or one simply needs to play more games.

Match play focuses on combining skills into a real life situation where match game goals may be style specific, such as learning to play against a certain style. The goals could also be focused on learning to using a specific tactic through a shot combination, or perhaps learning to transition between shots, or utilizing specific footwork elements.

> *"It is important to always vary the training methods so that the training models the shots and combinations that will be encountered during a real match"*

Training goals are much more specific and deliberate. They focus on a predetermined set of shots and are aimed to developing proper response or movement in a controlled environment. Without controlling the environment it is difficult to build consistency through repetition. Yet controlling the environment the same way all the time can adversely impact anticipation and footwork. Now, instead of reacting to the ball, instinctively producing the desired response, an automatic subconscious, familiar response takes over and performs the same activity as the one engraved through heavy repetition.

Therefore, the concept of overtraining a specific skill comes into light. It is important to always vary the training methods so that the training models the shots and combinations that will be encountered during a real match. One must always make note of the shots that are causing them the most trouble during the matches to be able to clearly identify not only the type of shot that was received but also the combination of strokes that led up to that shot. Training against these difficult combinations or shots as they occur will first help develop awareness and anticipation of what is happening during the point. Proper responses practiced during training will eventually begin to automatically surface during your match play.

It is therefore important to identify which part of training is focused on a mere warm up, and which part of training has a specific goal. Once goals are achieved, new goals or refined goals can be established in order to continue improving.

I urge you to ask yourself questions regarding your training as often as you can. The more you examine and evaluate your training, the more you will be in control of your development and the faster you will improve.

Without a purpose, there is no goal. Without a goal, there is no need for training. Without training there is no improvement. Without improvement, your dreams are a mere fantasy.

Take control of your goals by simply aiming to achieve one small goal at a time. Once it is attained, create a next goal, and then another. Small steps will yield great results, I promise you!

Proper service strategy

I have already covered service training and the proper time for bringing service training exercises into your daily training routine. This chapter will address the next element of training: understanding the purpose of the serve and how to create a proper service strategy in the game.

I came across this topic when I was around USATT 1600 level. I found myself struggling to initiate an attack against certain opponents. While I used my serves quite well with other players, new players returned my serve in a way that did not allow me to initiate an attack and win the point as I had anticipated. I was constantly caught unable to make a strong opening.

What I failed to realize playing against my opponents was that I was simply using the wrong service strategy. Prior to reaching USATT 1600 level, it was safe to serve the ball long and I could almost always expect a push in return regardless of the type of serve I was using. Because my opponents produced the same predictable response to all of my serves, I was always ready to attack an underspin ball. Higher rated opponents were much more experienced and did not push the ball all the time. Since I did not serve a short ball, they were able to comfortably spin the ball. Returns when my opponents spun the ball frustrated me. I wanted a push in order to attack, but was receiving a slow spin shot which was difficult to read both in terms of the spin on the ball and its placement. I began to alter serves to deliver stronger side and top spin service combinations attempting to intimidate the opponents and force them to push, but instead, I was attacked even harder. I lost many games before my faulty strategy was identified was corrected.

> *"...players must always be aware and prepared for the best possible and safest responses to their shots."*

The main reason I was experiencing this difficulty in my game is because I was not aware of one very basic rule of table tennis: table tennis players must always be aware and prepared for the best possible and safest responses to their shots. This is especially true for service. I anticipated one type of response, but my opponents who were delivering a different shot - halting me from making the proper attack shot to the incoming ball and taking full initiative in the point. I was simply over anticipating.

When I finally began to make adjustments, I became a prey to my own strategy. I was not realizing that long serves were enabling my opponents to start their own opening. I felt safe since my opponents were not attempting to crush the ball with a loop drive. I had a false sense of security. Hence, when my opponents returned the ball with a soft touch, I attacked a slow, soft, sometimes lightly padded ball with the same shot as I would attack the underspin ball. Having the weapons for a strategy to attack an underspin ball well, I was attacking a no spin or top spin ball with the same shot, frequently making an unforced error.

My whole service strategy required an overhaul. In training, I had to learn the types of responses to anticipate from my opponents for *all* variations of my serve. It was no longer enough to put the ball in play and "go from there." I had to pause to get ready for a serve and visualize what would be my opponent's proper response. Then, I had to go over the proper stroke to use against such a response. In addition, new training elements needed to be addressed in this step. I needed to expand my third ball training to attack flips with the same merciless attack as the attack of a push.

To summarize, remember that a short underspin serve will produce an underspin push as a response most of the time. Side spin serves will come back with side spin using a push or a topspin with a flip. Topspin serves, whether short or long, will come back as loops or flips, unless you are playing a defensive player. Expecting these types of shots as the service return will make it easier for you to develop the proper strategy against your opponents and take your game to the next level.

Timely backhand development

My coach is well known for his strong backhand. Every time I heard someone talk about my coach's game, I heard admiration regarding this particular shot.

www.breaking2000.com

Gerald has a hell of a forehand as well, yet for some reason it is always the backhand that comes to stick to Gerald's opponents mind when they are talking about his game. I could not explain this phenomenon until Gerald and I began to develop my very own backhand.

Today, Gerald is proud to pass his torch over to me as the player with a good backhand. While my backhand technique is quite different than his own and it is personalized to my style, it is a skill that has really helped separate me from other USATT 1800 level players, finally allowing me to take my game to the next level and reaching USATT 2000.

"It is important to work on the backhand side in order to keep the strength of backhand strokes in balance with the strength of the forehand. Otherwise, the differences in the strength of backhand and forehand wings will become too obvious, allowing the opponents to build their strategy around the weaker side"

Gerald and I began to work on developing an offensive backhand soon after I broke USATT 1600. He noted that very few players of my level or at even higher levels worked on the development of their backhand. Gerald was absolutely correct in his observation, and the lack of training of the backhand side is visible at higher levels even more so than it was before. Most people focus on strengthening their forehands and choose to run around the table trying to use the forehand. Meanwhile, players with strong backhands have better defense and attacking opportunities.

It is important to work on the backhand side in order to keep the strength of backhand strokes in balance with the strength of the forehand. Otherwise, the differences in the strength of backhand and forehand wings will become too obvious, allowing the opponents to build their strategy around the weaker side. In addition, since not too many players have the patience and determination to develop a better backhand, early development of the backhand will allow the player to reach farther up the skill level in a shorter amount of time.

There is another reason why a player needs to begin to work on the backhand a lot sooner in their development: most players simply struggle developing this particular shot. Elements of timing, footwork, and reading of the incoming ball's placement and spin are difficult to learn. The backhand cannot exist on its own and needs to be as dynamic and skillful as the forehand. Transition between backhand and forehand shots in a combination needs to be perfected in order to avoid gaps in open, attacking game. Finally, backhand needs to be tied well into the service return and 3rd ball attack. This type of training also needs to cover the use of the backhand as a tool to bring a strong forehand loop drive into the game.

With the many applications of the backhand stroke, a developing player must pick the proper time to commit to learning the use of the backhand. Remember that learning the backhand means giving up a strong forehand for a little while until the backhand has fully matured. Yet, I urge every developing player to surrender the wish for a killer forehand temporarily for the greater good - improved balance between backhand and forehand shots, improved backhand defense, and overall stability of the player's game.

For me, backhand became my main weapon allowing me to beat many penhold and defensive players. I no longer needed the extra time to run around using my forehand on every shot and was capable of forcing my will on an opponent sooner using a wider selection of shots and angles available by combining the forehand and the backhand shots into combinations. Building a backhand capable of generating more spin and power than my forehand was, incidentally, yet another benefit. If I could attribute my breaking USATT 2000 to one particular skill, it would be to the backhand. This is the shot that allowed me to gain the final 200 points I needed to reach this level. Without it, I would be just another fast but predictable forehand oriented USATT 1800 looper.

Selecting the right coach

The toughest task in developing yourself as a player is choosing the right coach. The scarcity of coaches makes it an impossible task for players residing in certain parts of the country. These areas of the country may not have any coaches for miles. Therefore, I will write this section assuming that there are coaches available in your area.

Selecting the proper coach is a very challenging task. Compared to other countries that have numerous government sponsored table tennis programs, players in the United States are forced to purchase coaching time on their own. This is where the importance of finding the right coach is even more critical. Players need to learn the material as quickly as possible due to get the best return on investment. Table tennis training lessons are not cheap, and therefore the training needs to be timely and efficient.

> *"Your coach should be actively engaged into proactive development and have good foresight into the steps needed to develop a good player including creation of a proper training plan and performing routine game analysis to measure the ongoing progress."*

I was lucky to meet Gerald. I have met many other coaches whose numerous students, despite many years of training, have been unable to improve. This is why I would like to address several principles of coach selection that I recommend to all new table tennis players.

First and foremost, I recommend setting specific expectations for every lesson. I value my time and money and want my training to be specifically aimed to accomplish something, even if the skill in question is not fully developed in one session. This allows for the tracking of progress and makes planning the next training session more effective. Your coach should be actively engaged into proactive development and have good foresight into the steps needed to develop a good player including creation of a proper training plan and performing routine game analysis to measure the ongoing progress.

> *"One of the key questions to ask your coach during any lesson is 'Why?' This question is the source of all the knowledge that combines the routine training into a game."*

If not offered outright, ask your coach for a reports and training plan changes on regular basis, especially after milestones in training or tournament results have been achieved. Coaches prefer to be informal, but any words can be forgotten and misunderstood. Having a solid plan on paper allows planning and development to be measurable and thus attainable. Players that set specific goals for themselves should want to control and measure their improvement, rather than simply waste time and money to let the training follow its own unguided course.

One of the key questions to ask your coach during any lesson is "Why?" This question is the source of all the knowledge that combines the routine training into a game. Without proper understanding of the purpose of the exercise, a student may not be able to suggest a better alternative for training. For example, if the student feels that he or she needs to work more on attacking underspin, but the coach recommends working on attacking a topspin ball, there needs to be a discussion why topspin training is should be taking priority over other skills. Deciding and agreeing on the skills that will be learned or improved will be beneficial for the player.

Lastly, a proper system of training and feedback needs to be established between a player and a coach - a system that allows for analyzing the game and its continuous development in order to better plan the next steps of improvement. This will keep the player and the coach actively engaged to achieve the same goal.

If it is possible to establish such a relationship between the coach and the player, the improvement will only be a matter of time. Failure to do so will likely result in a waste of both time and money, hence leading to a lack of commitment from the coach, lack of trust from the player, and a lack of results on the court.

You can take your own progress into your own hands by keeping track of the skills you need to develop, the training you perform, and the results you achieve in tournaments. Use your coach to help you find the right way to solve problems in the way you apply your technique and in the way you use strategy and tactics, and your improvement will be full of purpose and results.

Rating skills matrix

This section summarizes the skills one needs to possess in order to advance in table tennis. Some players may go up a level by learning or strengthening a different skill that the ones listed below. This list is meant to be a guide rather than be set in stone. This is the skills matrix that allowed me to improve from level to level during my quest to USATT 2000.

USATT 1000

- Decreasing overall count of unforced errors
- Resisting the desire to make wild shots
- Focusing on producing spin on shots as opposed to power
- Developing proper technique of basics strokes
- Building consistency of countering shots

USATT 1200

- Learning vary placement of serves
- Ability to attack high and long service returns
- Not rushing the shots
- Controlling the point of contact of the ball on the paddle
- Achieving high repetition of basic countering shots from both forehand and backhand (at slower pace)

- Perfecting technique of basic strokes by being able to execute basic strokes multiple times in a sequence

USATT 1400

- Producing short serves
- Controlling push from both wings
- Ability to open up an attack against a push with slow spin
- Ability to open up an attack against a higher push with a power shot
- Improving footwork in order to open an attack against first possible push (learning step around the backhand, also called pivot rotation)
- Development of a 3rd ball attack on the forehand

USATT 1600

- Backhand block
- Improved control of a push on service return
- Backhand attack of a long serve
- Improved service return of side spin serves
- Shortened strokes for quick recovery and repetition
- Consistent spin of a pip or anti ball
- Development of a flat hit on the forehand side
- Improvement of backhand and forehand transition
- Ability to loop down the line and crosscourt with the forehand with same consistency and power

- Retaining 3rd ball attack consistency while controlling the placement of the attack, aiming to attack wide angles
- Mental training – retaining focus, playing hard when the games are close
- Understanding strategy

USATT 1800

- Backhand block consistency
- Backhand punch
- Backhand attack of an underspin ball
- Learning to attack long tomahawk and pendulum serves with force on forehand and backhand
- Improved consistency in continuous attack against choppers and retrievers
- Smashing a lob
- Developing consistency in topspin to topspin countering on the forehand
- Solid 3rd ball attacks on forehand and backhand
- Development of a 5th ball attack (particularly developing proper transition from attacking underspin and topspin ball in succession)
- Forehand and backhand transition close the table and at mid distance
- Development of side spin forehand loop – designed to drive opponent away from the table
- Mental training – fighting and winning most close games
- Improving strategy by learning to find opponent's weaknesses and aiming to expose them

- Solidifying all openings against long and half long serves – opening shot must be positive (attacking, not passive)
- Service and service return training – aiming to open against any loose serve
- Mental training
- Solidify strategy – early discovery of weaknesses and learning to win points by attacking a weakness with a tactical combination
- Controlling pace and spin – ability to alter between slow heavy spin loops and fast power loop drives
- Learning to increase the spin of a no spin ball or underspin ball coming from pips or anti defender
- Learning to counter on the backhand
- Controlling backhand block placement – ability to block the ball wide and down the line.
- Mastering 3rd ball attack using wide angles
- Footwork improvement – ability to maintain good balance during large distance movements to the ball and away from the ball (such as when a cross over point is attacked requiring the player to move away from the ball to make room for a stroke)
- Developing the physical tolerance to retain positive play in a long rally. Mental focus must be maintained as well.

Hopefully this matrix explains the types of skills that need to be learned in order to advance between these levels. One thing to note is that when moving up a level, the material of the previous level must be mastered with a high level of consistency since all other skills are built on top of the foundation set up in the previous level.

There are no shortcuts! Most important aspect is to continue working on perfecting the skills and increasing the difficulty of training as you advance into the next level.

In addition, if development stagnates, go back to refine the skills learned in the previous level prior to taking on more advanced material. This allows you to reset the basics to prepare for further improvement.

Learning off the court

Achieving USATT 2000 was not an easy task. I spent many hours working out on the court. I spent even more hours off the court reading, researching, and watching. I feel that even with a great coach, my goal would not have been attainable if I did not spend a lot of time reading table tennis books and researching many other table tennis topics.

The same is true for any player. Several hours of private coaching a week do not suffice to cover all of the material you need to know to be successful in this enormously complex game. There are nuances in every shot because every shot has many dimensions – spin, speed, power, placement, height, risk, control, and finally mental pressure. There are just as many elements in training – controlling each of the above listed dimensions can be aimed to be perfected during a training session. However, all of these elements simply cannot be learned all at once.

Table tennis is just like any other discipline – knowledge of high level table tennis can only be acquired after learning the lower level game. Being impatient and seeking to find the answers to many of the questions helped me discover tons of information that benefited me along the way.

Besides reading more about the sport and its heroes like Jan-Ove Waldner, Ma Long, Timo Boll, Wang Liqin, Wang Hao, Ma Lin, Vladimir Samsonov and many, many others, more time needs to be spend on mental preparation. Many materials exist on preparing an athlete for a better performance. I have read many books and utilized the methods described in the books to improve my mental game. Without this training off the court, I would still be struggling to compete against my peers.

> *"I urge you to take every opportunity you have, whether on the court or off the court as a chance to learn and a chance to improve."*

Finally, I spent many hours shadow practicing and practicing touch simply bouncing the ball on the paddle while watching TV. All of this off the court training kept my mind zeroed in on my end goal, and every exercise I executed brought me one step closer to achieving my goal.

I would like to share one secret that really inspired me to reach my goal and break 2000 USATT when I was stuck in a plateau unable to break out of USATT 1800. I began writing this book. I felt that putting the initial touches of my ideas on paper was yet another effort I could initiate off the court to help me break out of the stagnation I was experiencing at the time. It was a mental reinforcement that really boosted my morale. I urge you to take every opportunity you have, whether on the court or off the court as a chance to learn and a chance to improve.

If you are like me and have a strong desire to succeed, treat every minute as a minute that can be spent on table tennis training. Even with God given talents, only hard work can help someone achieve their desired goals in this game. As my coach says: "This game is not for weak of heart."

It is not about points

Throughout this book, I have mentioned ratings and rating levels many times. This is probably the best way to compare the skill level of various players within the USATT member community. It especially helps understand the skill differences between a player in one level and a player in another level. Yet, the rating points have no other value. While USATT 2000 sounds like a nice round number, every player should approach their own number subjectively.

> **"Ratings points do not define a player. Player's skills define rating points through results produced in competitive tournament level settings."**

Rating levels do not make up a player. There are skills that some lower rated players can execute extremely well. These players should be commended! Some of these players could be just a few skills away from jumping not one but several levels up in their game. Therefore, I urge the reader never to be focused on rating points. Ratings points do not define a player. Player's skills define rating points through results produced in competitive tournament level settings.

> **"Rating points are not worth anything and therefore should have no take in your game play. If you are truly better, you will beat your opponents."**

Therefore, when training, aim to develop your skills and your rating points will follow. Do not be afraid to play lower rated players because rating points are at stake. Rating points are not worth anything and therefore should have no take in your game play. If you are truly better, you will beat your opponents. Failure to win must not be treated as a disappointment either – it must be treated as a free lesson which exposes yet another element in the game that you can work on improving.

Playing against better players, you must have the same mentality. Do not be afraid to compete against better players. As long as you give it your best and play your game the way you have been practicing it, there can be no embarrassment whether losing 11-0 or 11-9. Playing better players is always a measure – a measure of improvement.

> *"...there is no need to rush, there is no need to be disappointed and there is no need to ever doubt in your ability to win. There is just a need to find new weaknesses in your game and learn to turn the weakness into weapons."*

Even at this point, there are several players in my club that I have never beaten. I am certainly closer to them in rating points than I used to be, but this is irrelevant when comparing skills and experience. Slowly but surely my skills are becoming stronger. I am gaining invaluable experience in the process. I am certain that future wins against my club mates will come in due time. Nevertheless, there is no need to rush, there is no need to be disappointed and there is no need to ever doubt in your ability to win. There is just a need to find new weaknesses in your game and learn to turn the weakness into weapons. When the day comes and I begin winning against the best players in the club, I will know that I yet again improved and my level has yet again gone up.

In the meantime, focus on winning your tournament round robin group, your quarterfinal and semifinal matches, and lastly the final match – focus on becoming a champion and enjoy even the smallest of accomplishments achieved in the process.

It is *never* about the points…

The timeout

"Timeout!" I put my paddle gently on top of the table and head over to the bench. I pick up the towel, wiping the sweat off my hands and forehead, focusing on nothing more than a match. I have my eyes open, but I see the table and the match point play out in my mind that is about to come to life in front of all the spectators. I take a sip of water to clear my throat. It is a deuce in the 5th and I have the ad point. It is my turn to serve.

I head over to the table, thinking: "Nothing drastic. Easy does it, but if the opportunity is there, take it! You *know* what to do." I pick up the paddle and wait for my opponent, anxiously settling into his ready position. This is the moment I've been waiting for. Here comes the toss…

Just like any basketball player shooting to score a point at the buzzer, just like a football player trying to fly over the line for a touchdown with fractions of a second left on the clock, just like a baseball player swinging at the ball with bases loaded during a last inning with two outs and two strikes, I wanted to be the one to score the last point of the match against my opponents.

Two years and four months have gone by before I could proudly say I won enough of matches to break USATT 2000, and I feel that any player with dedication to his goals can do it too. It's not a magic mark, it is attainable with proper tools, the talents, and hard work. I hope this book serves as one of the tools to help you map your own path to success and guide you in time of need throughout your quest. I hope I gave you the inspiration to make up your goals and confidence that you can reach them too.

Some say I am talented. Some say I am extraordinary. Some say I am lucky. I do not believe that I am any more talented than anyone else who plays this game seriously. I also definitely do not believe myself to be extraordinary. But I am lucky. Lucky to have found a great coach, lucky to been born with several inner virtues - a strong need to succeed, an ability to commit fully to my goals, and a lot of dedication. Everything else is the result of hard, constant and sustained work.

If you are just like I am, an aspiring table tennis player with a strong desire to excel and succeed, if you are observing and admiring USATT 2000 players and would like to join their ranks, I have one piece of advice for you: do not give up. You can reach this level too.

In the meantime I take a timeout as I am going to attempt to reach yet another level: USATT 2200. I hope to get there just in time to tell you how I did it....

March 8, 2011

Appendix

USATT Rating results for are posted on USATT web site: www.usatt.org.

Below is the direct link to my history profile:
http://www.usatt.org/history/rating/history/Phistory.asp?Pid=63749